AF471161

AMEDEO MODIGLIANI

ediciones polígrafa

masterpieces

AMEDEO MODIGLIANI

© 2005 Ediciones Polígrafa, S.A.
Balmes, 54. E-08007 Barcelona
www.edicionespoligrafa.com

© Text: Manuel López Blázquez
Translated from the Spanish by Alberto Curotto
Color separation: Format Digital (Barcelona)
Printed and binded at Mateu Cromo (Madrid)

Available in USA and Canada through D.A.P./Distributed Art Publishers
155 Sixth Avenue, 2nd Floor, New York, N.Y. 10013
Tel: (212) 627–1999 Fax: (212) 627–9484

ISBN: 84-343-1068-6
Dep. legal: B. 10.385 - 2005 (Printed in Spain)

All rights reserved. No part of this publication may be reproduced in any form
or by any means without the prior permission in writing by the publisher.

CONTENTS

7 ON THE FRINGES OF THE AVANT-GARDE

11 AMEDEO MODIGLIANI, 1884-1920

16 SELECTED BIOGRAPHY

18 SCULPTURE

26 THE QUEST FOR A PERSONAL LANGUAGE

35 FACES

52 NUDES

59 THE PARISIAN BOHEMIA

78 LIST OF WORKS

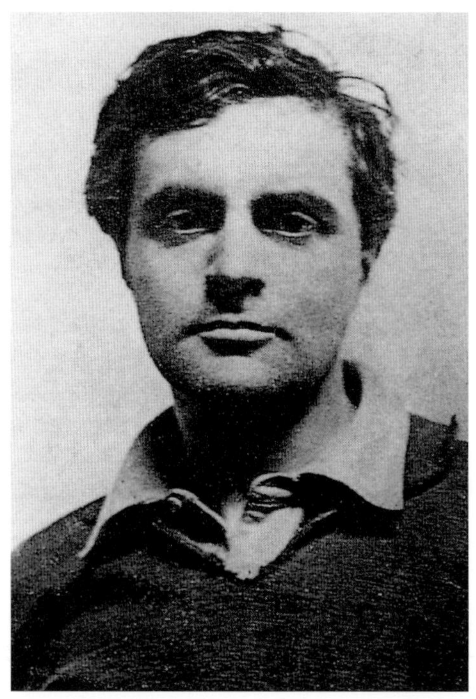

Modigliani, *c.* 1914

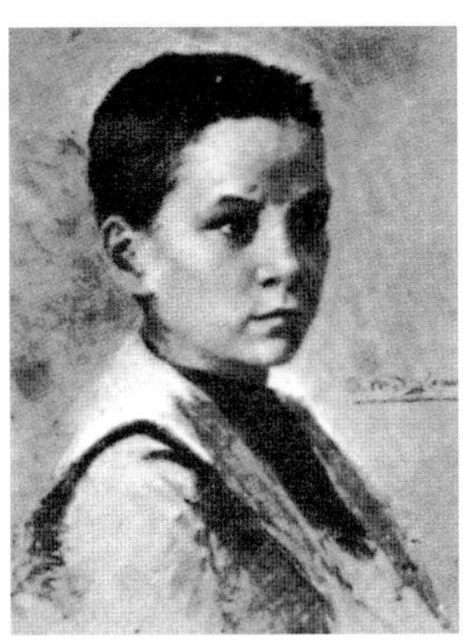

ON THE FRINGES OF THE AVANT-GARDE

"Dédo," as his parents used to call Amedeo, executed this surprisingly expressive self-portrait when he was only fifteen. In this charcoal drawing he timidly approximates the "dash of color" *(macchia)* technique typical of the Macchiaioli, a group of Tuscan painters whose work foreshadowed some of the key elements of Impressionism.

The art scene during the first two decades of the twentieth century was almost single-handedly shaped by the groundbreaking emergence of avant-garde groups. In this climate, Modigliani was yet an eccentric figure, belonging to what—for lack of a better label—has been called "Ecole de Paris." The only thing the members of this group shared, aside from their physical ties to the French capital—which historian Giulio Carlo Argan once noted served as the center of the international art market rather than the seat of any particular school—was their rejection of academic impositions, as well as a common aspiration toward modernity, a goal rooted in the intellectual and aesthetic premises set forth by the artistic movements of the late nineteenth century. It was in this cosmopolitan setting, frequented by artists from every corner of the world, that Modigliani would develop his own peculiar style, and his works—like those of Marc Chagall or Constantin Brancusi—are proof that, in 1915, it was quite possible to be a modern artist without being enlisted in any particular avant-garde movement.

CREATIVE FREEDOM

Modigliani did not share the strong associative drive of his contemporaries. His own relationships with other artists—such as Utrillo, Soutine, Foujita, and Kisling—were not based on a sense of aesthetic affinities as much as on close personal friendships. His well-known refusal to accept painter Gino Severini's invitation to endorse the first Futurist manifesto in 1909 was not motivated simply by his independent ambitions, but rather by his own strong ties with

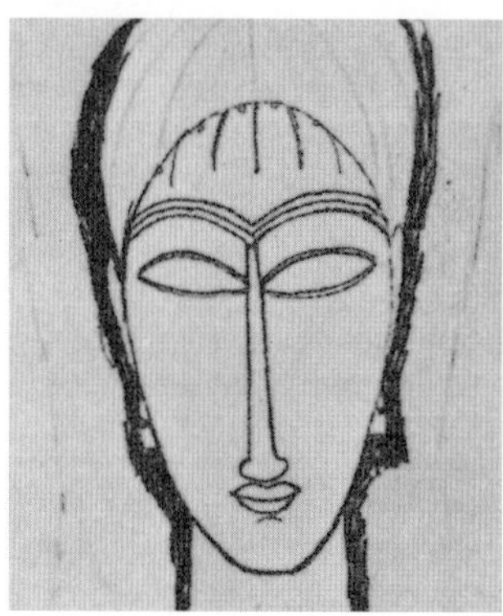

tradition. For the Italian artist, the iconoclastic rants of his countrymen—whose scorn for art would eventually lead them to advocate, among other things, the destruction of all museums—could only induce contempt. From the outset—with an attitude inherited from his Macchiaioli teachers—Modigliani rejected all academic influences, resolving to assert his own creative freedom and autonomy.

BETWEEN PAST AND FUTURE

The Parisian lifestyle had a modernizing effect on Modigliani's artistic evolution through a number of different influences, from his awareness early on of Toulouse-Lautrec's and Paul Gauguin's emphasis on the decorative aspect, to the chromatic revolution launched by the Fauvists as a result of Paul Cezanne's crucial insights into the constructive value of colors. Nonetheless, Modigliani's works would continue to display traditional references. His production bespeaks the inspiration of Italian trecento artists—such as Simone Martini and Tino di Camaino—as well as of the art of ancient Egypt and of archaic and primitive civilizations, which by then were beginning to be studied throughout Europe. Modigliani's relationship with ancient art was far from nostalgic; rather it was grounded in the harmonious application of artistic procedures. Like the Khmer artist or the Egyptian sculptor, Modigliani filtered data through a process of abstraction—in the literal sense—capturing the essence of the motif through his own subjectivity and poetic nature. This method required the artist to establish an emotional connection with his model, a type of focus that excluded all physical surroundings in the studio, and yet

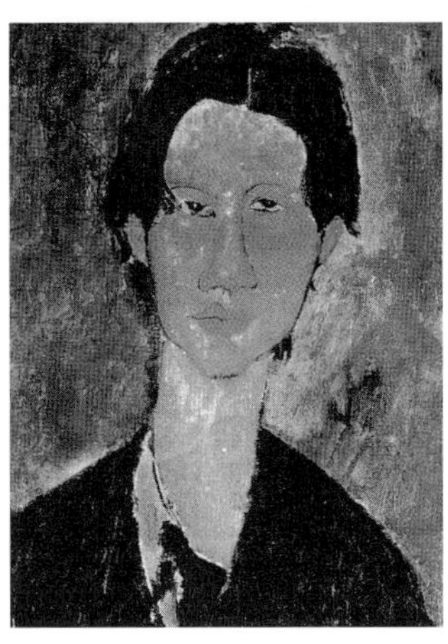

was likely to last only until the end of any one sitting. This may well be the reason why, for the most part, Modigliani painted his works in one day without interruption. Modigliani was receptive to the varied stimuli generated by the many avant-garde groups of the time, and this, along with his desire to reconcile these novel approaches with his traditional leanings, made him a precursor to the spirit that animates some of the artistic currents of today. While the avant-garde movement may be officially defunct, it aided in formulating new, partial, and nonexclusive readings of the modern tradition. Poised as he was between past and future—a peculiar condition to which French poet Guillaume Apollinaire had drawn attention early on—Modigliani's work therefore possesses a timeless quality, one that actually prevented its public recognition and success in an age when novelty was becoming in itself a quality of tantamount importance. By the same token, however, the subtle elegance and seemingly monotonous quality of his work, with its delicate refinement, was bound to become the very key to its later success.

A ROMANTIC ARTIST

The popularity enjoyed by Modigliani's work posthumously has no doubt been bolstered by the myth surrounding the artist, a myth that the painter himself helped to create and that was further enhanced by his untimely death. A man of impressive good looks and countless lovers, passionate and defiant and yet hampered by illness, Amedeo fits perfectly into the role of the Romantic artist. According to a description by Jean Cocteau, "a dark fire kindled his entire being, radiating through the fabric of his clothes and conferring on his slovenly figure a certain dandyish air. He was joyful, witty and charming." Some of his contemporaries, though, felt that his attitude smacked of the poseur. Ever the caustic wit, Pablo Picasso—for whom Modigliani held a profound but unrequited admiration—is said to have expressed surprise at the fact that the Italian artist made a scene with his alcoholic ravings only where they would most likely be noticed: on the corner of boulevards Montparnasse and Raspail, at the very heart of the Parisian artistic bohemia. Whether he was posing or not, Modigliani's attitude was fostered as a young man, when his readings of Friedrich Nietzsche and Gabriele D'Annunzio had persuaded him of the exceptional nature of the creative artist: an individual—as Modigliani once wrote to his friend Oscar Ghiglia—who, in view of his different needs, is entitled to special rights unlike those of other mortals.

Ironically, Modigliani's underlying elitism, which focused its distaste on the bourgeoisie, was nurtured along with his profound responsiveness to the plight of the human condition, as evidenced by a statement inscribed on one of his drawings: "Life is a gift / from the few to the many / from those who know and who have, to those who know not and have not." Even though he had seemingly chosen to live a poor existence—indeed, his mother gave him money throughout most of his life—Modigliani nonetheless suffered severely from his lung illness and was certainly not indifferent to the lack of recognition his work received. Despite such vicissitudes, however, his artistic production remained impervious to the slovenly aspects of his existence and firmly rooted in its delicate, melancholy world.

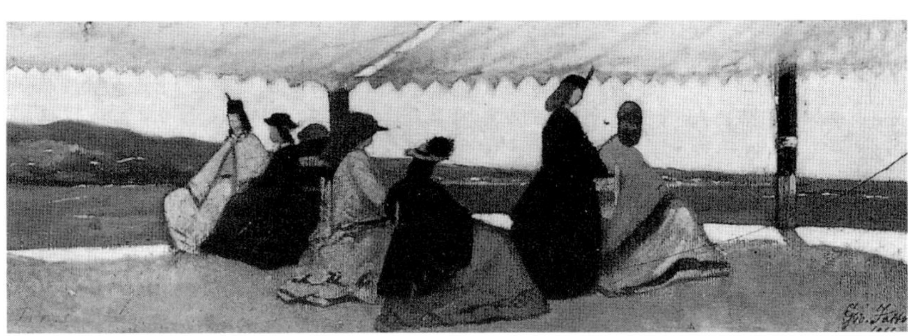

Giovanni Fattori, THE PALMIERI
ROTUNDA, 1866. Modigliani
discovered Fattori through
the latter's pupil, Micheli,
who, like his teacher, was torn
between a more Romantic style
and the realism of the "dash of
color" technique practiced by
the Macchiaioli school, to which
both painters belonged.

AMEDEO MODIGLIANI, 1884-1920

Amedeo Modigliani was born in 1884 in the Tuscan city of Livorno
(also known as Leghorn) to a relatively well-to-do family of
Sephardic Jews. He was the youngest of four brothers, the eldest of
whom, Emmanuel, was destined to become a prominent leader
of the Italian Socialist Party. Their parents were Flaminio Modigliani,
a businessman of Roman origins, and Eugenia Garsin, an educated
and open-minded woman who played an extremely irfluential role
in shaping the character of the young Amedeo. Two events occurred
in his early life that were to permanently irfluence him thereafter.
At age fourteen, he contracted a serious case of scarlet fever, from
which he never fully recovered, and then two years later he began,
with his mother's consent, to take drawing lessons. In her diary,
Eugenia confessed that she saw in this activity a way for her
son to overcome the "listlessness" resulting from his illness.
Modigliani was fortunate in that unlike most of his bourgeois
colleagues, he never met with his family's antagonism regarding
his artistic pursuits.

ART FEVER

In 1898, Modigliani gave up his regular course of studies and began
to frequent the studio of Guglielmo Micheli, a pupil of Giovanni
Fattori's and, like the latter, a follower of the Macchiaioli—a group of
painters from Tuscany whose "dash of color" technique foreshadowed
certain aspects of Impressionism. During the winter of 1901,
Modigliani came down with tuberculosis and, in pursuit of a warmer

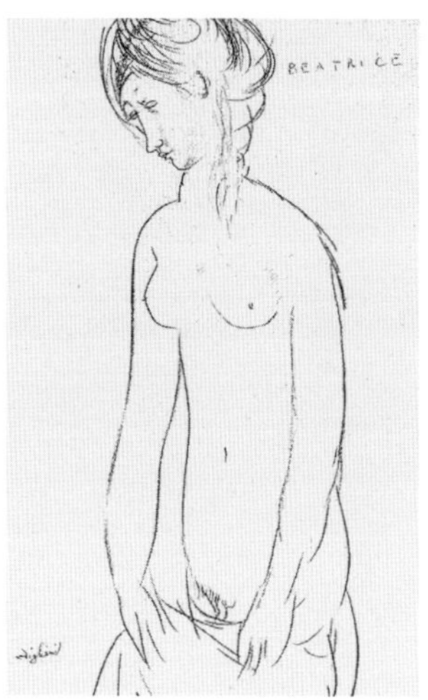

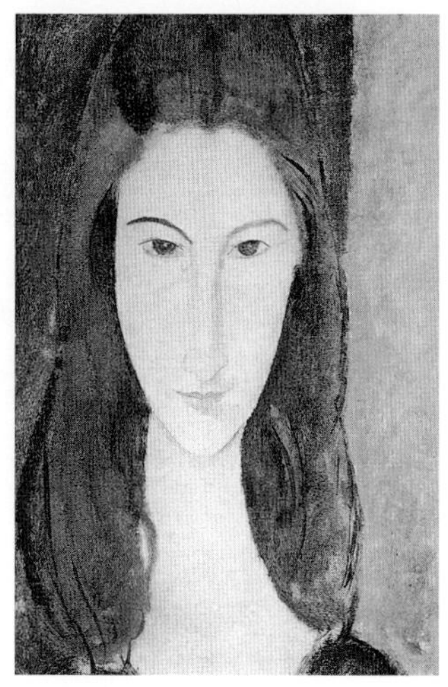

climate, traveled to the south of Italy with his mother. The journey
enabled him to experience firsthand the great works of Italian art,
rekindling and confirming his desire to become an artist. In 1902
he enrolled at the Accademia di Belle Arti (Scuola Libera di Nudo)
in Florence and, the following year, at the Instituto di Belle Arti in
Venice. There Modigliani met the Chilean painter Ortiz de Zárate (who
would eventually become his neighbor in Paris), to whom he confided
his desire to become a sculptor. It was arguably here in Venice that
Modigliani, emancipated from his family's protection, first began to
leed a bohemian lifestyle, attending occultist séances and using
hashish. These Venetian years can be viewed as a rehearsal for his
trip to Paris, where he arrived early in 1906, and where he rented
a studio on the rue Caulaincourt in the district of Montmartre.
Soon thereafter he enrolled at the Colarossi Academy and began to
carve stone sculptures, obtaining the necessary materials—rather
hazardously—from a number of Parisian construction sites. Always
neatly groomed in his velvet suit and scarlet scarf, Modigliani plunged
into a city that was then experiencing its zenith as an art center: the
Fauvists had recently caused a sensation at the Salon d'Automne
of 1905, and Picasso was already working on his *Demoiselles
d'Avignon,* the revolutionary painting destined to become the seed
of Cubism.

A BOHEMIAN IN PARIS

Even though the Italian artist early on became one of the most
distinctive representatives of the city's bohemia, he always remained
on the margine of any more or less organized movement. In 1907

he met the man who would become his first mentor in Paris: Paul Alexandre, a physician who had established a small community of artists in a squatter building on the rue Delta. The following year, Alexandre persuaded Modigliani to show some of his works at the Salon des Artistes Indépendants. While all six paintings seemed predominantly irfluenced by Cézanne, Modigliani's work through the end of the decade also showed signs of Toulouse-Lautrec, Gauguin, and Picasso's Blue Period.

SCULPTURE

In addition to Dr. Alexandre, the other most influential figure in the development of Modigliani's artistic career was his neighbor at the Cité Falguière in Montparnasse, the Romanian sculptor Constantin Brancusi. Modigliani had never really given up on his desire to become a sculptor, so in 1909, he decided to devote himself entirely to this artistic medium. His works from this period, which lasted until 1914, were done in the stonecutting method and resulted from a process of stylization heavily indebted to African art—a subject of profound fascination for most avant-garde artists of that time—as well as to the statuary of both ancient Egypt and archaic Greece.
In 1912 his friends, appalled by the painter's deplorable living conditions, decided to chip in and collect enough money to send him home, hoping that in a more familiar environment he would amend his bohemian habits. Thus, in the summer of that year, Modigliani traveled for the last time back to Livorno, in his native Italy, where he was soon able to locate a studio and resume sculpting. According to some unconfirmed biographical lore, the criticism of his friends

toward his work may have induced the artist to fling his own
sculptures into a local canal (known as the Scali Olandesi), which to
this dey have never been recovered. This trauma, together with the
lack of a studio better fit for carving stone, and the detrimental health
effects that breathing stone dust had on his weak lunas led Modigliani
to give up working in sculpture once and for all. Nevertheless, this
phase of the artist's career was characterized by intense exercises in
synthesis that left their mark on his later production. In 1914, at the
outbreak of World War I, Modigliani's failure to enlist in the army
because of his delicate health allowed him to resume painting
with a renewed vigor. His Parisian friends continued to be the main
supporters of his work, among them the art dealer Paul Guillaume,
who bought some of his paintings and replaced Dr. Paul Alexandre
as a mentor when the latter left to fight in the war; the South African
poet and journalist Beatrice Hastings, with whom the painter had a
troubled romantic relationship; and, above all, Leopold Zborowski,
a Polish poet who in 1917 became both Modigliani's close friend
and art dealer.

A TRAGIC ENDING

Modigliani's first solo show, held at the Berthe Weill gallery in
December 1917, was closed down by the police on account of
some nude paintings— deemed immoral—that were on display in
the gallery window. Not a single work was sold. That same year
Modigliani met Jeanne Hébuterne, a nineteen-year-old woman who
would become his last companion and who bore the painter's only
acknowledged child, also named Jeanne. During that period, when

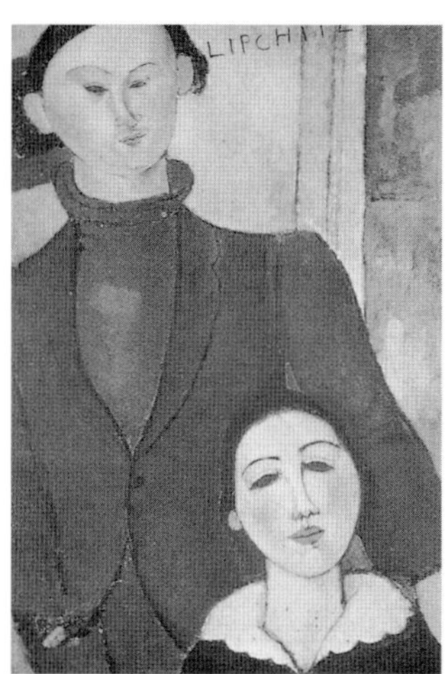

PORTRAIT OF JACQUES LIPCHITZ AND HIS WIFE, 1916-17. The Italian artist had a lifelong association with sculpture. In this painting, Modigliani has portrayed the famous Lithuanian-born sculptor Jacques Lipchitz, one of his friends from the Parisian bohemia.

the artist's works finally, albeit slowly, began to sell, his health took a turn for the worse, and he became increasingly addicted to drugs and alcohol. In 1920, wasted by kidney disease and tuberculosis and after a week of suffering—during which the couple never left the painter's studio, nor sought assistance from the outside world—Modigliani died in a Parisian hospital. Within a few hours, Jeanne, who was already in the ninth month of her second pregnancy, committed suicide by jumping from the window of her apartment.

1984 He is born on 12 July in Livorno and named Amedeo Clemente Modigliani. He is the fourth and last child of Flaminio Modigliani and Eugénie Garsin. Flaminio is from an old Jewish family from the village of Modigliani, south of Rome, and runs a small money-changing business. Eugénie is from a bourgeois Sephardic Jewish family from Marseille. Emanuele, Amedeo's older brother becomes a socialist member of the Italian Chamber of Deputies. His sister Margherita never marries but brings up Jeanne, Modigliani's daughter.

1894 Amedeo goes to school (the *ginnasio*) in Livorno. Prior to this, he is taught at home by his grandfather and one of his uncles on his mother's side, both of whom are well educated and interested in the young boy's personality. Flaminio is absent much of the time and his business collapses.

1895 Amedeo suffers from pleurisy. He continues his secondary studies at school until 1898.

1898 He suffers from typhus that leads to pulmonary complications. While ill and feverish, Amedeo dreams of his path in life, art. When he recovers, he enrolls at the School of Fine Arts in Livorno, joining the studio of Micheli. He passes his baccalaureate.

1900–01 He is diagnosed with tuberculosis. In the winter, his mother takes him in search of a warmer climate to southern Italy, in particular Naples, where he visits the Capodimonte Museum, Capri and Rome.

1901–1902 Following a visit to Florence, Modigliani spends the winter in Rome with the financial help of his uncle Amédée Garsin, whose business affairs in Marseille are prospering.

1902 He returns to Florence. He enrolls at the Scuola Libera di Nudo (Free School of the Nude), where he studies under Giovanni Fattori. He is captivated by Renaissance art.

1903 He goes to Venice, where he joins the Scuola Libera de Nudo of the Regio Instituto di Belle Arte of the Venice Republic. He strikes up a friendship with Manuel Ortiz de Zárate. He visits the Biennale and dreams of becoming a sculptor.

1905–06 Towards the close of 1905 or early 1906, Modigliani arrives in Paris, moving first into a hotel and then later into a studio on Rue Caulaincourt in Montmartre. He studies nude drawing at the Académie Colarossi on Rue de la Grande Chaumière. He becomes friends with he painter Maurice Utrillo (1833–1955).

1907 Thanks to the painter Henri Doucet, he frequents the artists' colony set up by the young doctor Paul Alexandre on Rue du Delta. Modigliani never lives in the colony's house but Alexandre becomes his first patron through his purchases of works of art or by arranging commissions for portraits from among his relations. Modigliani visits the Cézanne retrospective, though his own paintings are inspired more by the style of Toulouse-Lautrec.

1908 He shows five paintings and drawings in the Salon des Indépendants, including *The Jewess*. He leads the life of a bohemian in Montmartre.

1909 He returns to Livorno for a while, where he paints *Beggar of Livorno*. He meets the sculptor Constantin Brancusi through Paul Alexandre. It is not long before he moves to Cité Falguière, in the 14th *arrondissement*, near Brancusi, who has found a studio for him there.

1910 Modigliani shows six works in the Salon des Indépendants. In the Cité Falguière, he devotes himself exclusively to sculpture, focusing on caryatids and heads. He becomes friends with the poet Max Jacob, with whom he shares a marked taste for spiritualism.

1911 He exhibits stone sculptures that he calls "columns of tenderness" in the studio of the Portuguese artist Souza Cardoso. He continues to explore the theme of the caryatid.

1912 He presents sculptures in the Salon d'Automne, one of which is bought by the Welsh painter Augustus John. He meets the sculptors Lipchitz and Epstein. At the end of the year, Modigliani goes back to live in Montmartre.

1913 He spends some time in Livorno in the spring. He works in marble, but none of his sculptures from this period have survived.

1914 The young art dealer Paul Guillaume, whom Modigliani meets through Max Jacob, takes Modigliani into his stable of artists and includes his work in a number of group exhibitions. He begins a passionate and stormy affair with the South-African-born journalist and poet Beatrice Hastings, the Paris correspondent for *The New Age* magazine. Guillaume rents a studio on Rue Ravignon for Modigliani. Modigliani devotes himself entirely to painting, though his canvases draw on his experiences as both a sculptor and a painter. Guillaume is called up to join the army in August. Modigliani, who also wants to enlist, is rejected on the grounds of ill health.

1915 Germaine Bongard, the sister of the couturier Paul Poiret, hosts an exhibition organized by Ozenfant. The artists showing work include Kisling, Picasso, Matisse, Derain, Léger, Severini and Modigliani.

1916 André Salmon organizes the Salon d'Antin at Paul Poiret's. Modigliani, who is by now painting multiple portraits of leading figures, is invited to take part. Following the end of his relationship with Beatrice Hastings, he spends some time living on Rue Joseph-Bara in the home of the Polish art dealer Leopold Zborowski, a friend of his.

1917 In July, he and Jeanne Hébuterne, who is also studying at the Académie Colarossi, set up home together on Rue de la Grande Chaumière. She is 19 years old. Her friends call her Noix-de-Coco (Coconut) because of the contrast between her extremely pale skin and her auburn hair. Her parents disapprove of her relationship with Modigliani. On the evening of 3 December, the very day of the private view of the only solo exhibition of his work held during his lifetime, the police order the Galerie Berthe Weill, where the exhibition has been mounted, to close on the grounds that the nudes on display are indecent.

1918 His tuberculosis begins to sap his strength and he goes to Nice with Zborowski, Jeanne, who is by now pregnant, and her mother. He makes frequent excursions to Cagnes-sur-Mer, where he meets Soutine, Survage, Foujita and Blaise Cendrars. A daughter Jeanne is born on 29 November. In December, a group exhibition entitled "Painters Today" is organized by Paul Guillaume. The artists included are Utrillo, Picasso, Matisse, De Chirico, La Fresnaye and Modigliani.

1919 Modigliani visits Auguste Renoir in Cagnes-sur-Mer, but is little taken with the confidences of the master, who likes to "caress the bottoms" of his models "for hours" before settling down to paint. When Renoir asks him for his opinion on his canvases, Modigliani leaves and slams the door behind him without saying a word. He returns to the studio on Rue de la Grande Chaumière. Jeanne Hébuterne is again pregnant. Modigliani agrees in writing to marry her as soon as he gets his "papers," probably in reference to his passport. His work shown in a group exhibition in London is adjudged to be a success.

1920 Modigliani contracts tubercular meningitis and dies on 24 January in the Hôpital de la Charité. On 26 January, Jeanne Hébuterne commits suicide by throwing herself out of the window of her parents' apartment on Rue Amyot.

SCULPTURE

The extraordinary quality of Modigliani's twenty-five surviving
sculptures makes it difficult to speak of his "thwarted ambition," as
the Italian artist undoubtedly had a tremendous desire to express
himself in this medium to a far greater extent than he actually
did. According to Ortiz de Zárate, as early as 1902 Modigliani had
confessed to him that he "painted only for lack of something better,"
since he continued to harbor strong aspirations of becoming a
sculptor. With this in mind, it is quite surprising that Modigliani never
considered any sculptural technique other than stonecutting, which
was most certainly contraindicated for someone who suffered from
a chronic lung condition, and for whom the fine limestone dust
must have been intolerable. In the beginning, these circumstances,
compounded by the high cost of the materials and the scarcity of
clients, kept the artist from devoting himself entirely to sculpture
until about 1909, when he met Constantin Brancusi. The Romanian
sculptor validated Modigliani's conviction in the superiority of carving
directly into the stone and introduced him to the stylized forms of
primitive civilizations, which Modigliani aptly harmonized with his
own early passion for Egyptian and medieval statuary.

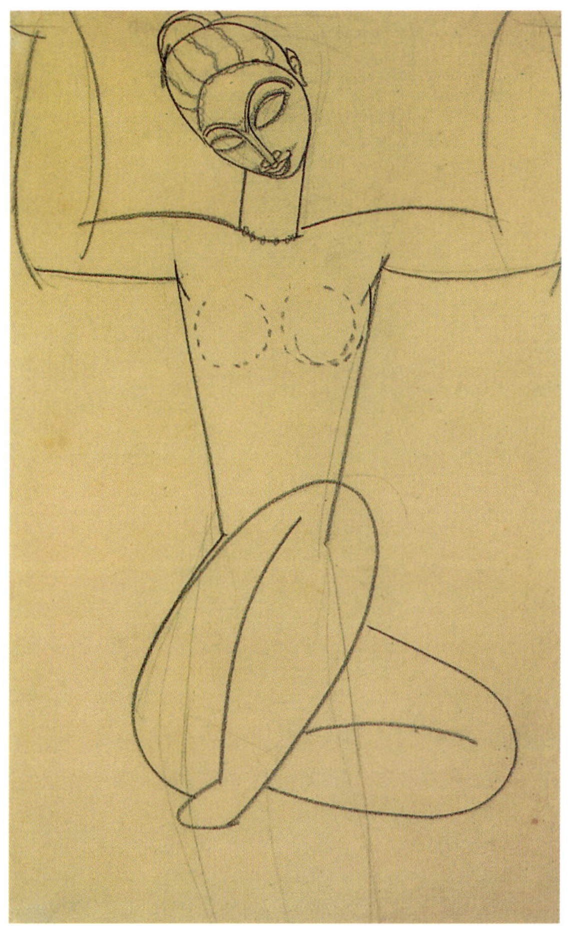

SEATED CARYATID, *c.* 1911. Modigliani's contact with primitive art was bound to leave a significant mark on his work, especially his concept of drawing: the chiaroscuro technique gave way to a supremacy of lines, which then became the dominant elements in compositions marked by extreme synthesis. In this drawing, in a Primitivist vein, the figure's features betray the direct influence of the Romanian sculptor Brancusi.

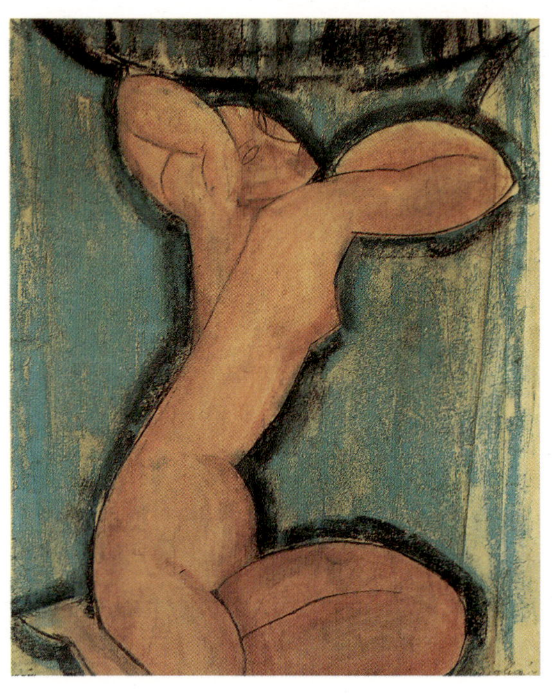

CARYATID, *c.* 1911; ROSE CARYATID WITH A BLUE BORDER, *c.* 1913. Modigliani's involvement with sculpture yielded a limited number of actual threedimensional pieces but a far greater quantity of prepatory sketches that, for the most part, bear the common title of "Caryatid." Indeed, they are preliminary studies for works that were meant to be incorporated into architectural structures, and their function as supporting elements justifies the figures' *contrapposto*, or contorted posture, that is equally reminiscent of Khmer temples and of Michelangelo's *serpentinata* forms.

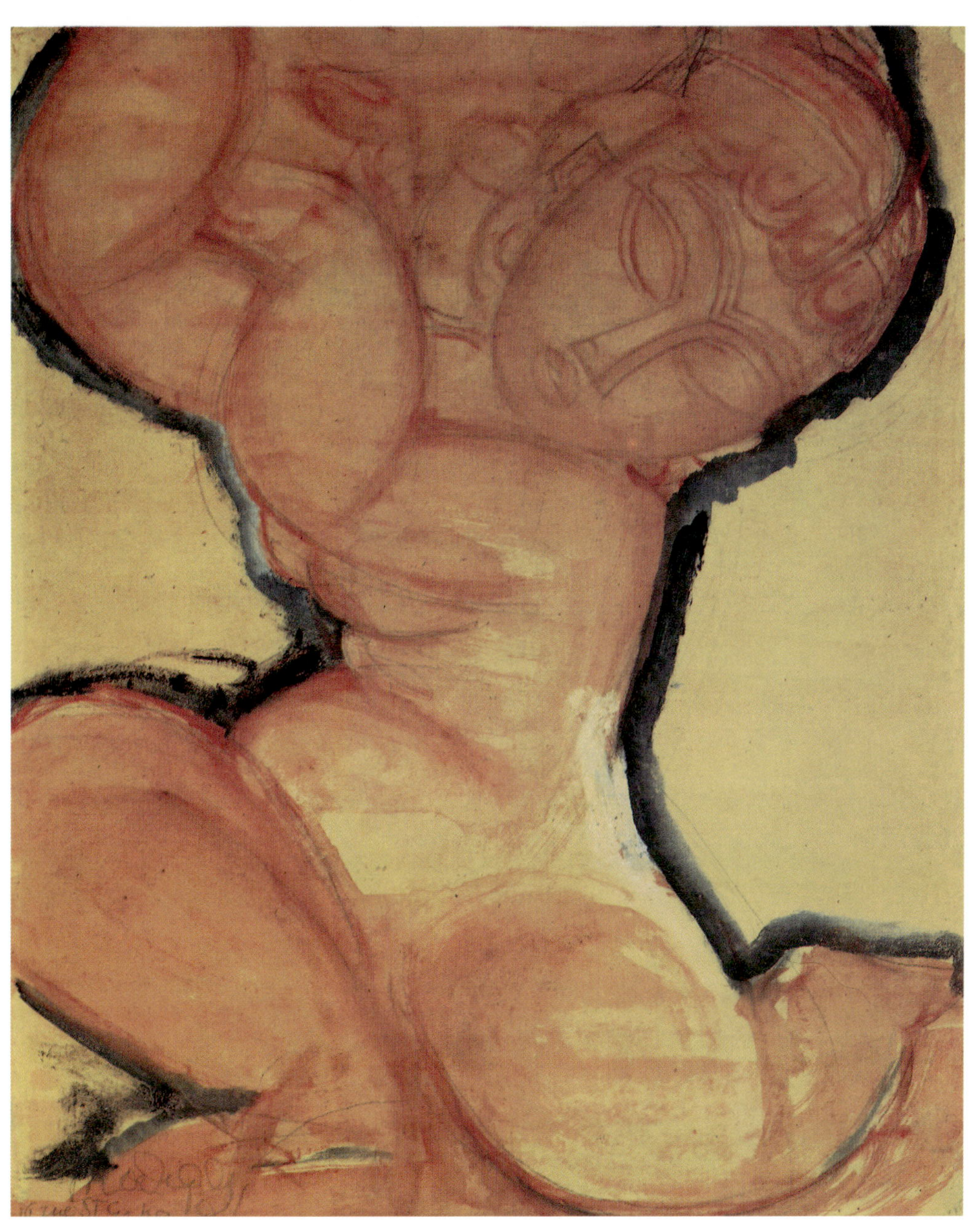

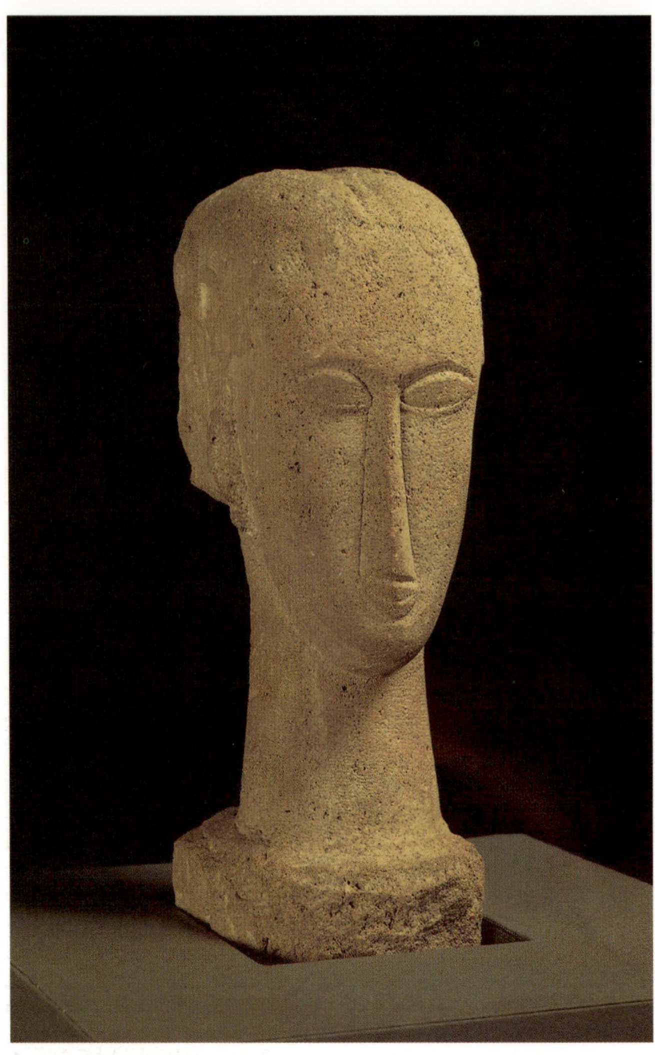

HEAD OF A WOMAN, *c.* 1911-12; HEAD, *c.* 1914. Modigliani's sculptures are the products of a creative process of synthesis. In view of his aesthetic quest for the essence of forms, it is possible that the Italian artist was strongly indebted to primitive art forms, as well as to the statuary of ancient Egypt, the Cyclades, preclassical Greece, and Romanesque sculpture. The simplicity of his style, however, has favored the proliferation of counterfeits. The most notable are the forgeries executed in 1984 by a group of students who claimed that they had recovered the "lost" sculptures Modigliani had supposedly thrown into a canal in Livorno. They succeeded in convincing most art critics of the authenticity of their discovery, and the farce continued until the authors of the fakes voluntarily confessed their deeds.

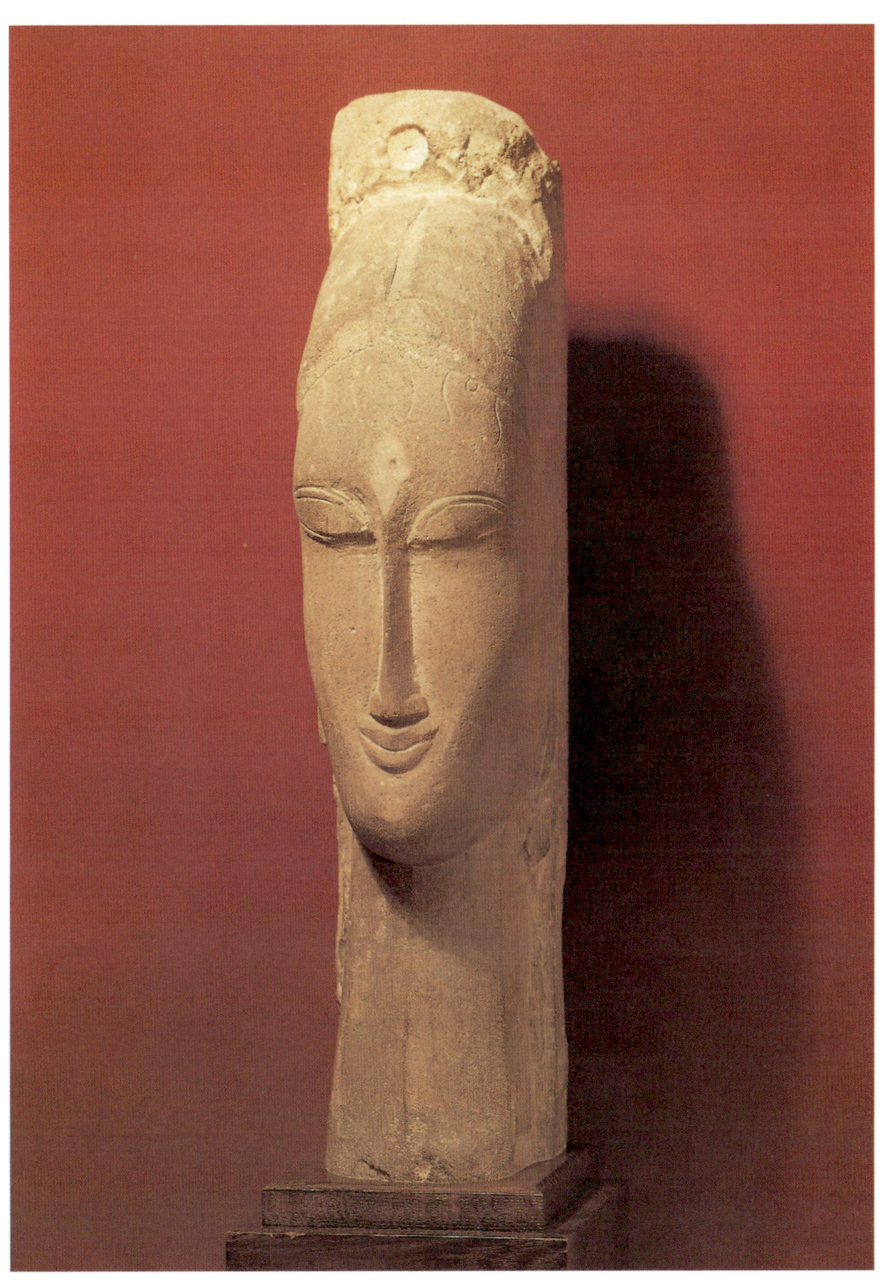

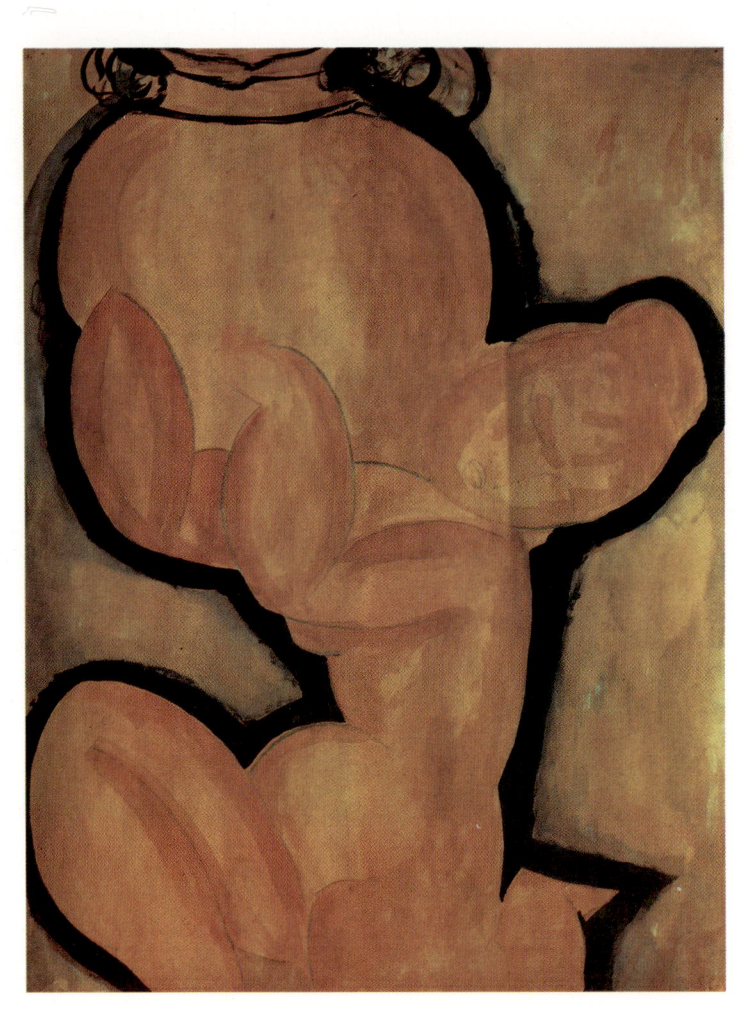

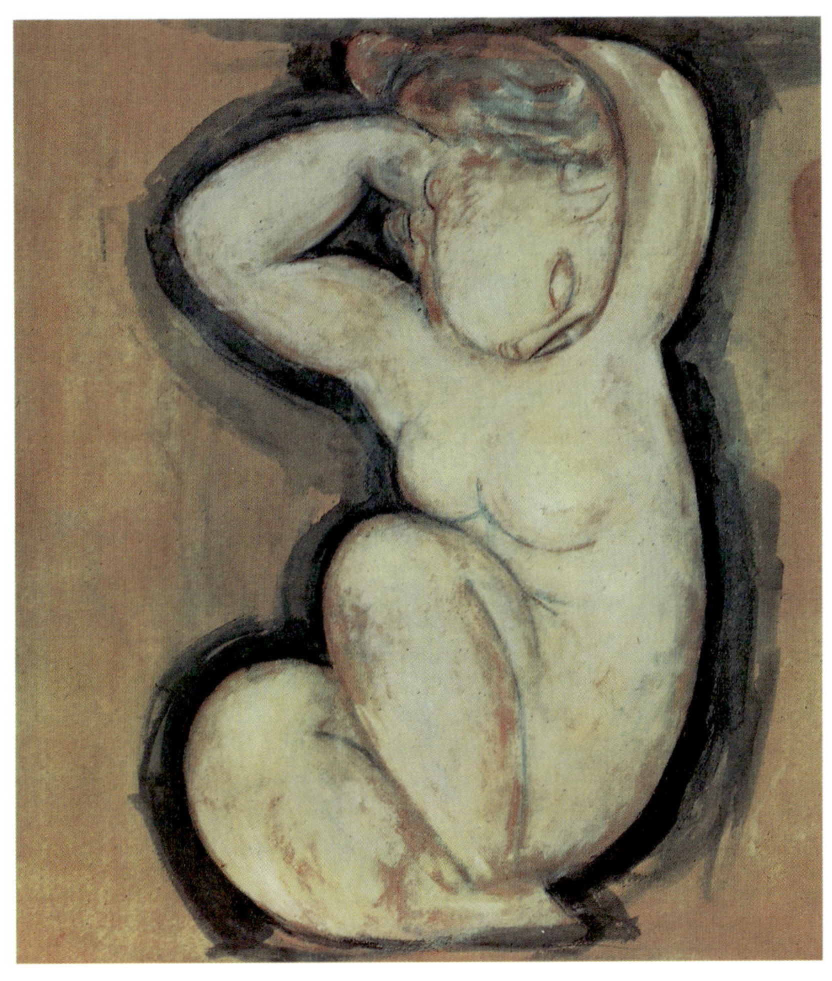

CARYATID, *c.* 1913-14; CARYATID, *c.* 1913-14. Modigliani's caryatids—only one of which was actually sculpted in stone—were meant to be, in the artist's own words, "the pillars of tenderness" of some utopian "Temple of Beauty." A temple that, as Paul Guillaume once stated, would rise "to the glory of Man rather than God, and would be crowned by hundreds of columns."

THE QUEST FOR A PERSONAL LANGUAGE

Modigliani's most distinctive and well known works belong to a very
brief period of his short career, from 1916 to 1920. Before then, the
technique of the Tuscan artist had experienced a number of different
influences and undergone substantial changes. Modigliani arrived
in Paris in 1906, and none of his early work survives, except a
charcoal self-portrait—executed at age fifteen—which though
technically rather conventional, is evidence of his early command
of draftsmanship. Ortiz de Zárate, a Chilean painter who had met
Modigliani in Venice in 1903, asserted that, in those years, the
production of the young Italian artist still had a rather academic
flavor. It was Modigliani's discovery of modern art that would
eventually bring about a profound transformation in his own
painting. The concurrent influences of Gauguin, Toulouse-Lautrec,
Picasso, and Cézanne are traditionally mentioned when examining
Modigliani's evolution as a painter; in fact, for a relatively extended
period, he alternated between all of these masters, but always from
an individual perspective. Indeed, the coherence of Modigliani's
artistic development contradicts certain statements made about
his career, such as Andre Salmon's claim that the Italian painter's
transformation from "diligent dauber" to "inspired vagabond"
occurred overnight.

PORTRAIT OF FRANK BURTY
HAVILAND, 1914. Modigliani's
definitive portrait of Diego
Rivera, along with this portrait
of the English collector Frank
Haviland, are the only two
surviving examples of his use
of a Divisionist technique.
The brushwork is fragmented,
producing in some portions
of the painting a discernible
pattern. However, the
intuitive nature of his work
is altogether alien to a
systematic application of
the Divisionist principies
of simultaneous contrast and
optical chromatic blend.

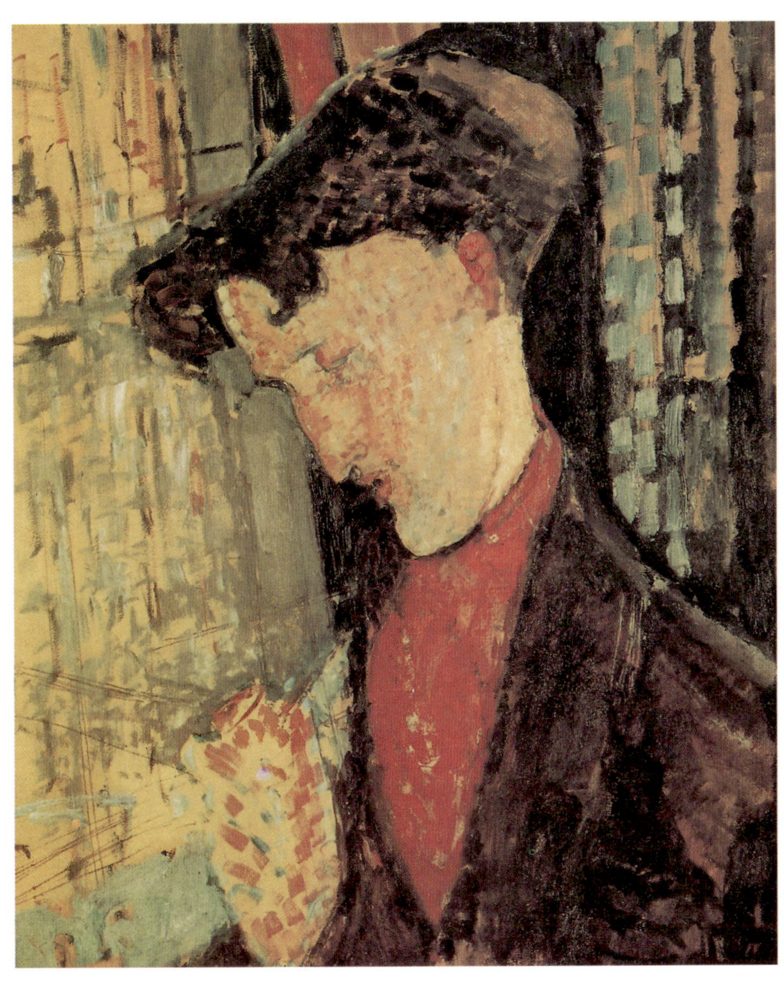

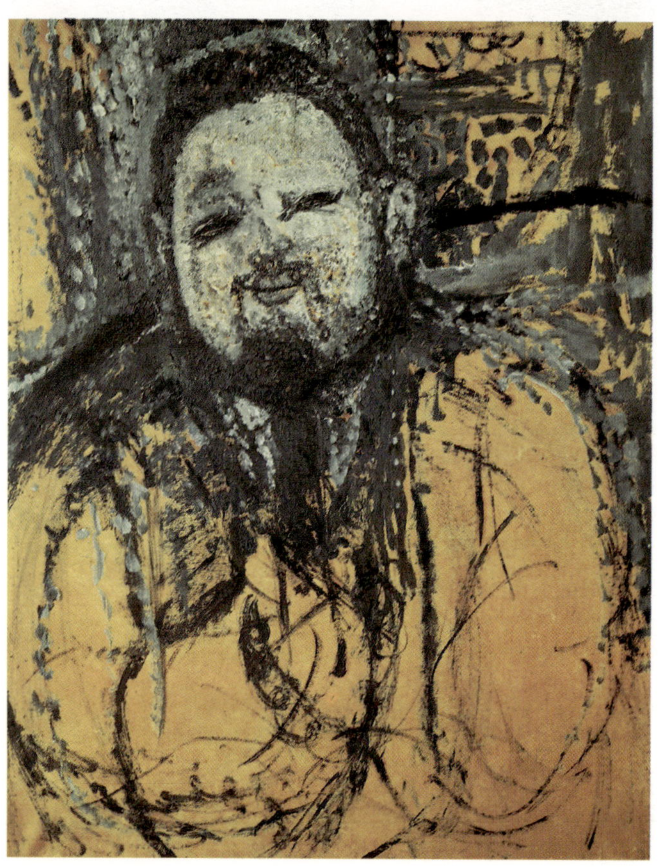

PRELIMINARY STUDY FOR THE
PORTRAIT OF DIEGO RIVERA, 1914.
At this time, the Mexican
painter Diego Rivera was one of
the most distinctive figures in
the Parisian bohemia. A fierce
polemicist and a hard drinker,
Rivera could often be seen at
a table in the café La Rotonde
in the company of such well-
known personalities as Leon
Trotsky. Modigliani portrays his
exuberant crony with a peculiar
blend of Pointillist brushwork
and more relaxed strokes,
highlighting the sketchlike
nature of this work.

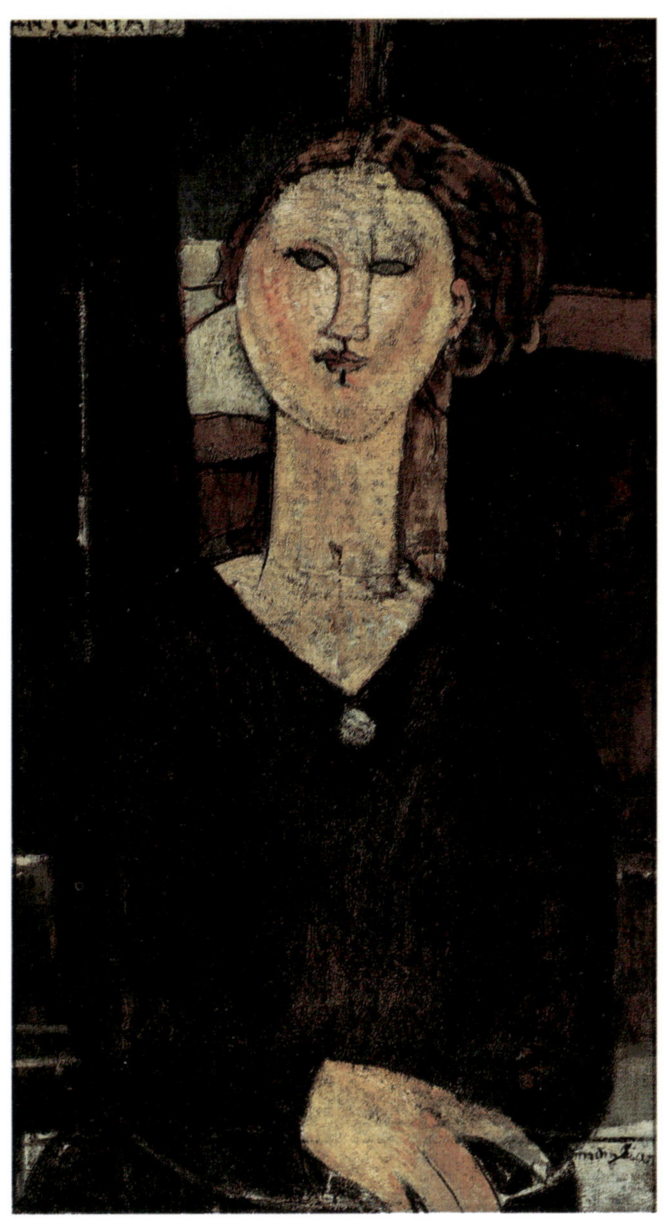

ANTONIA, 1915. As if in a rigorous application of Cézanne's maxim,
Modigliani constructed this figure from two basic geometric shapes:
the cylinder and the sphere. Yet, more than in the work of Cézanne,
the key to understanding this type of image can be found in African
art, which had a strong influence on Modigliani's work in the
period when he had taken up sculpture.

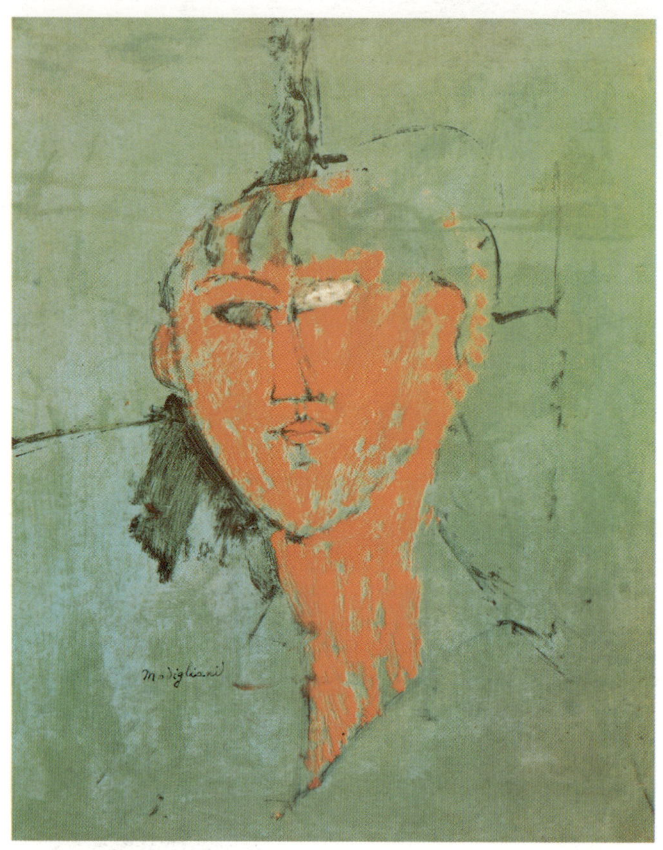

HEAD OF A YOUNG WOMAN, 1915.
Albeit rough, this sketch
reveals essential elements in
the artist's production in the
years immediately following his
interlude as a sculptor. The
spherical triangle of the head
is outlined by a thick black
stroke, which is also used
to delineate the asymmetrical
features of the face,
particularly the eyes and
the nose, while the mouth is
rendered as a diminutive spot
of deep red. As in many of
Modigliani's portraits, there
are two intersecting axes at
the head's center.

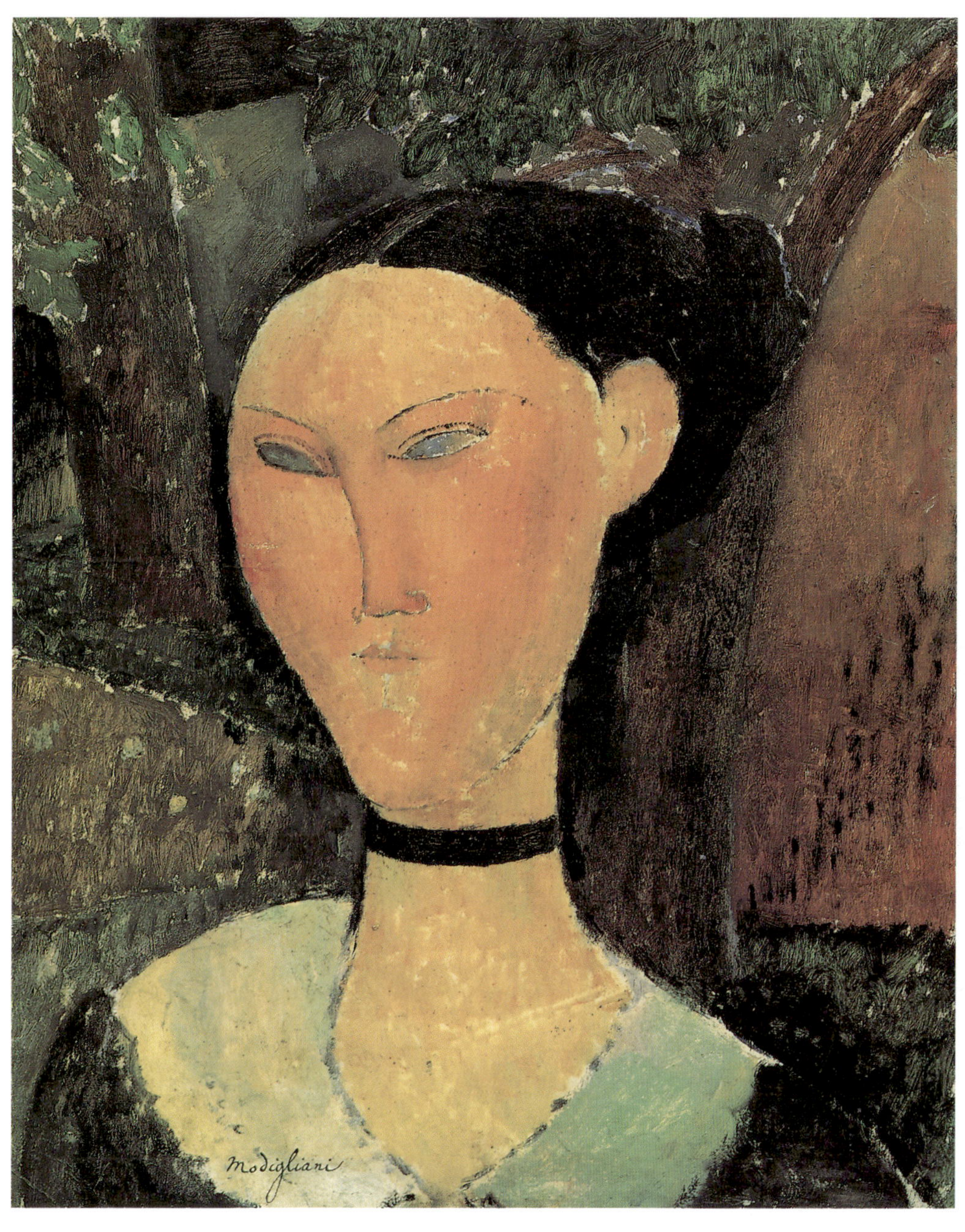

HEAD OF WOMAN WITH A VELVET RIBBON, 1915. This work is exceptional
in two respects: first, the sitter is portrayed in an outdoor,
organic environment rather than an interior one; second, the
treatment of that natural background is reminiscent of a tapestry
with clearly defined fields of color, much in the manner of the
"brickwork" typically found in works by Gauguin and the artists
of the Pont-Aven group.

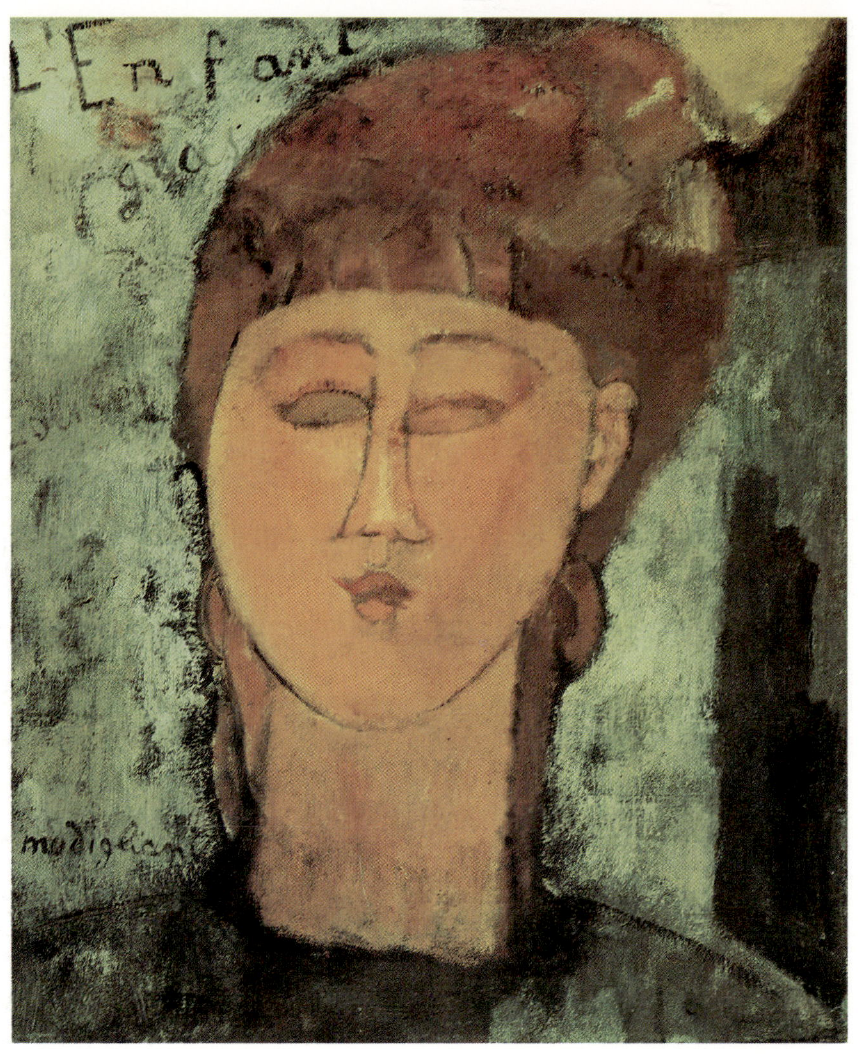

THE FAT CHILD (L'ENFANT GRAS), 1915. The title is inscribed
in the upper left corner of the painting. This stratagem, of
Cubist derivation, enabled Modigliani to deter any illusionistic
interpretation of the work, while at the same time underscoring its
autonomy as a self-contained object that is no less real than the
physical world to which it refers.

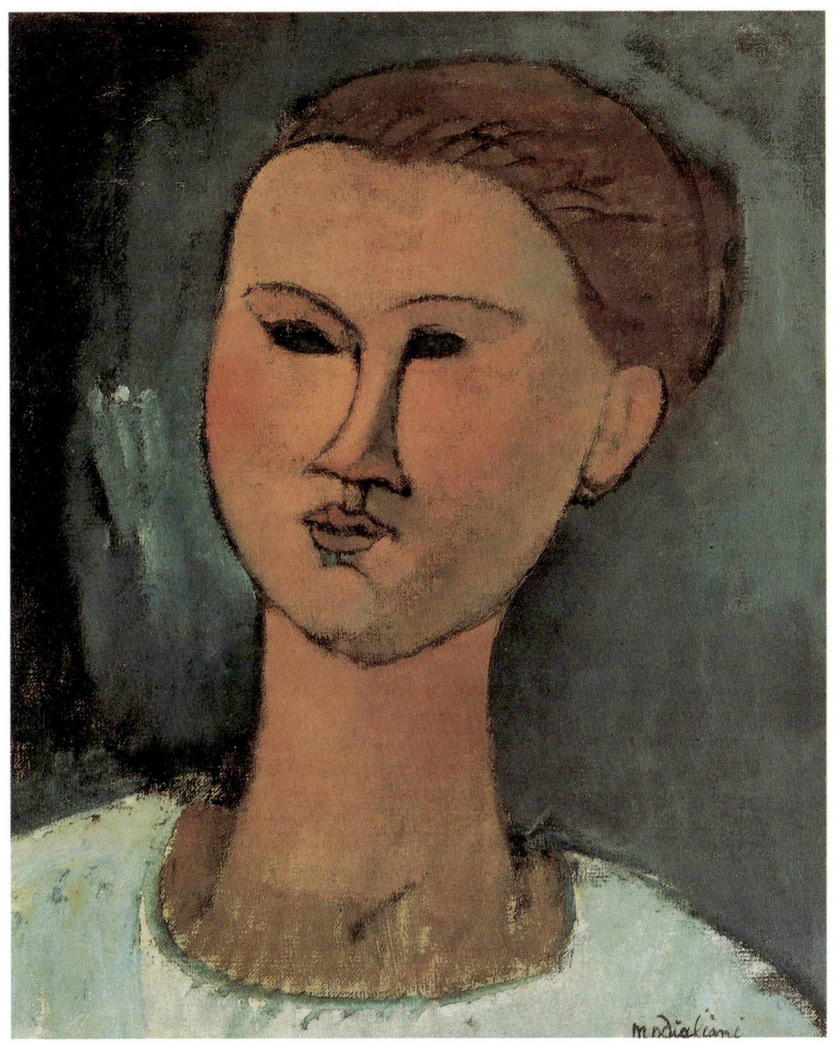

HEAD OF A WOMAN, 1915. This work evokes the process of synthesis Modigliani employed to create his figures after his stint as a sculptor. This manner of creation was heavily indebted to the art of primitive civilizations and, more directly, to Picasso. The distorted features of the girl's face, analyzed from different viewpoints, are reminiscent of the Spanish artist's bold treatment of the human figure in his painting *Les Demoiselles d'Avignon*.

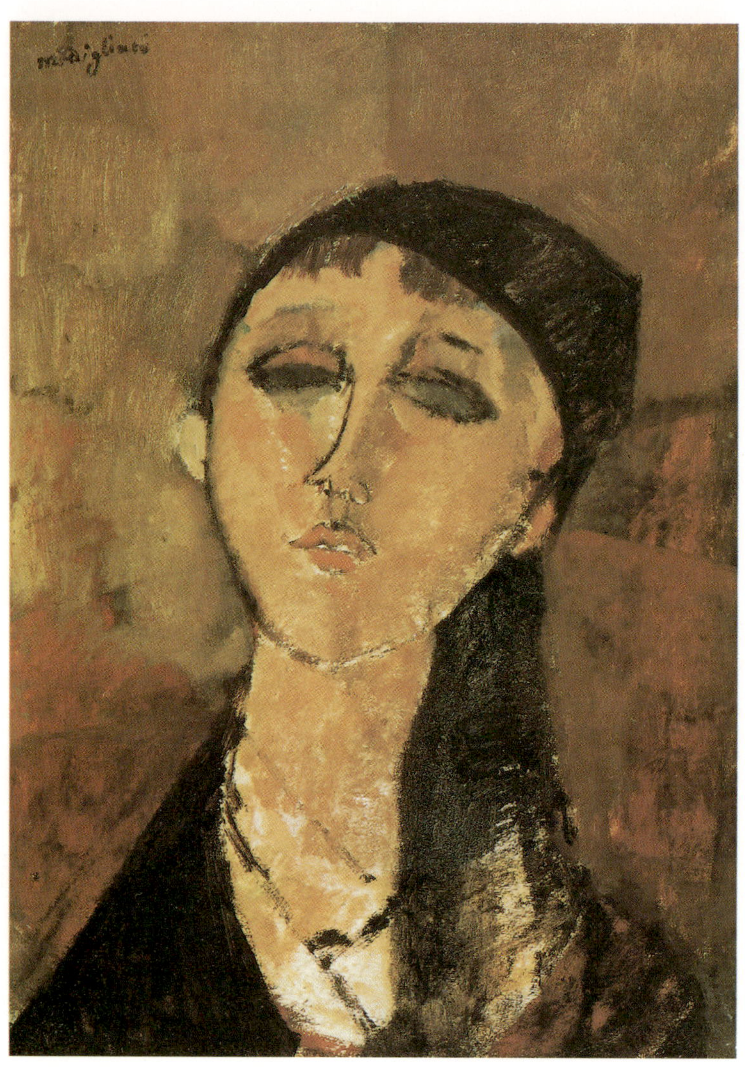

LOUISE, 1915. The infuence of Cézanne continued to be evident in Modigliani's works through the mid-1910s. Like the older master, Modigliani applied paint to the pictorial surface in a constructive manner, achieving a volumetric sensation by the juxtaposition of tiny spots of color. In this case, however, there are some other elements that are typically Modigliani's, such as the portrayal of the tilted head, the large vacant eyes, and the small, sensual mouth. All of this combines to invest this humble model with a distinctive air of acquiescence.

FACES

As one of his biographers pointed out, Modigliani's entire career was really a lifelong inquiry into the human figure. With the exception of four landscapes painted early in his career during a trip to the South of France—by the artist's own admission, "the work of a novice"—the human likeness is the only motif that really commanded his attention. Modigliani's portraits, executed for the most part in a single sitting, resulted from an intensely reflective process, requiring a strong emotional connection between the painter and his models. The latter were generally his friends or companions in misfortune, such as young apprentices, maids, and prostitutes. The portraits all share the same air of submissiveness, which most likely resulted not from the artist's alleged faith in the socialist doctrine of his brother, Emmanuel—as some critics have suggested—but rather from a sentimental affinity with the sitter. Most of these works share one peculiar element: the eye sockets are empty and uniformly colored, with no iris or pupil. Léopold Survage, unsettled by the portrait showing him with one normal eye and one dark, void socket, questioned the significance of such an anomaly, to which Modigliani replied: "With one eye you are looking at the outside world, while with the other you are looking within yourself."

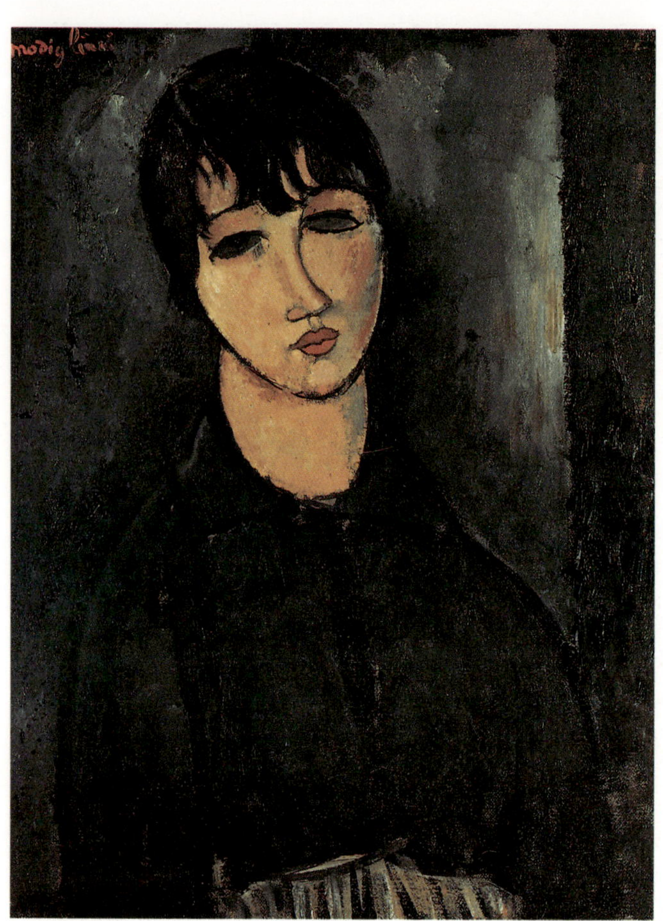

THE SERVANT, 1916. Modigliani
has depicted this domestic
woman's humble existence with
a sobriety that contradicts the
better-known sensuality of his
nudes. The young woman's body
almost blends into the cold
tonalities of her surroundings,
while the blue shadow on her
face—somewhat reminiscent of
Cézanne—only enhances her
expression of a resigned
melancholy.

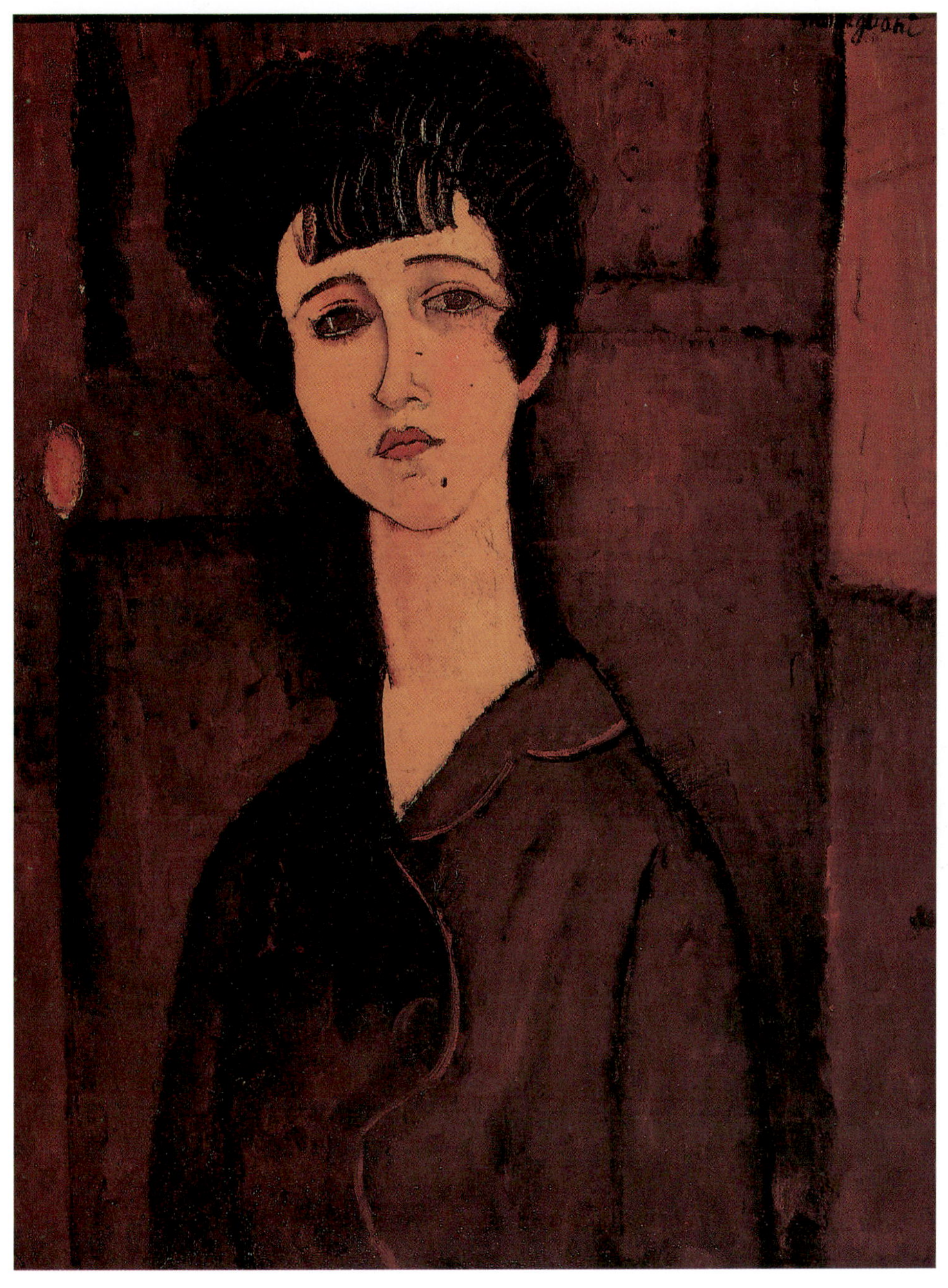

PORTRAIT OF A YOUNG WOMAN (VICTORIA), 1916. The portraits Modigliani painted during this short period are unusual in that in them he made an exceptional effort to accurately define the features of each sitter, hence the "conventional" representation of the model's eyes with clearly depicted pupils.

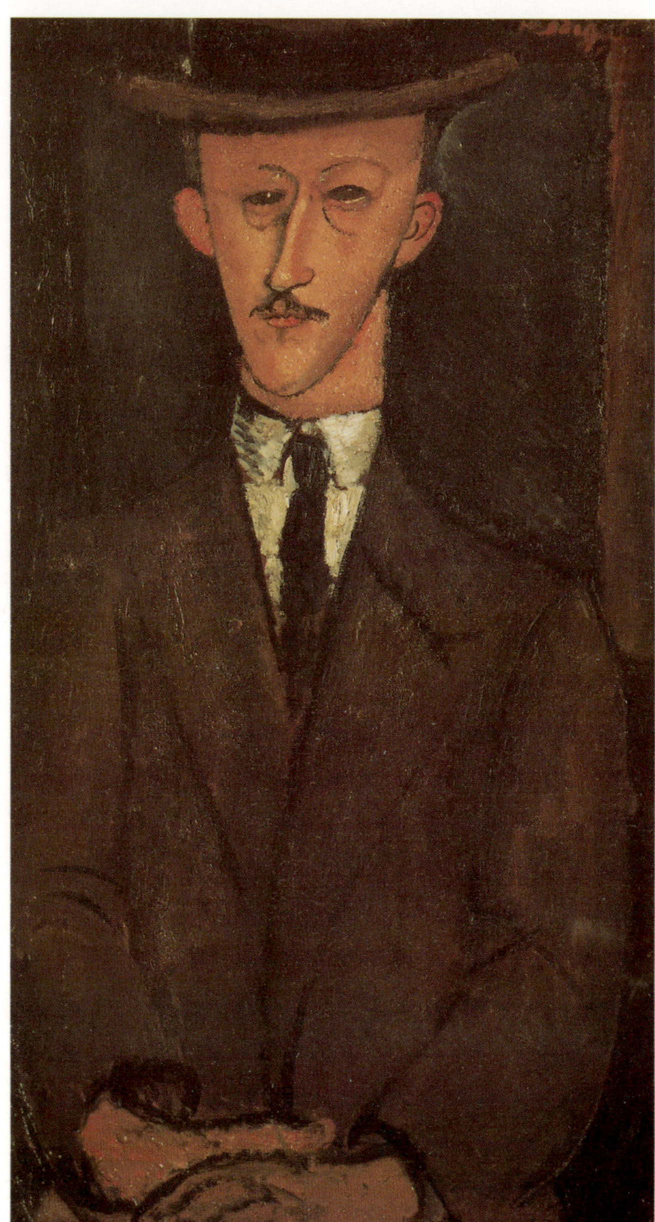

MAN IN A HAT, 1916. This painting clearly illustrates a consistent feature in Modigliani's production, namely the depiction of two different angles within the same portrait, showing how the frontal pose of the sitter's body melds with the lateral view of the same model's facial features. This intellectualized notion of anatomy is prevalent in primitive art and was given its ultimate expression by the Cubists.

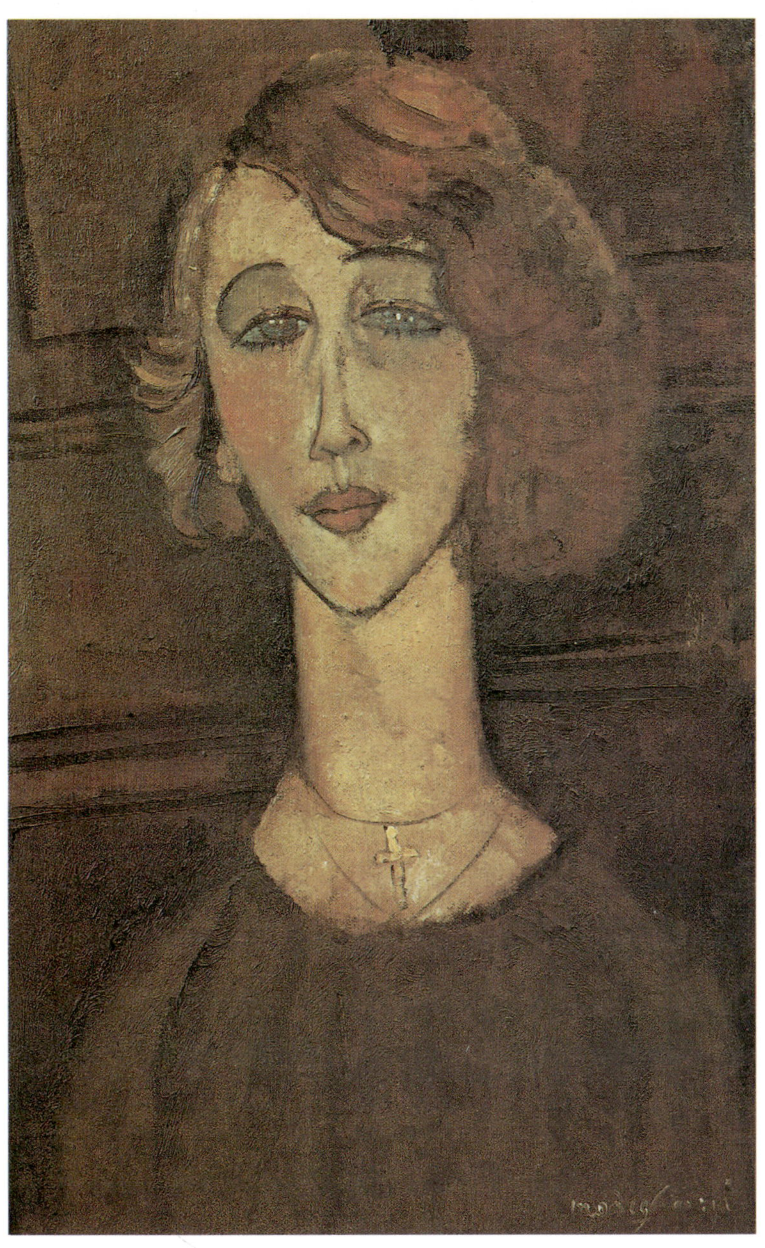

THE BLONDE RENÉE, 1916. Already in command of un exceptionally individual style, Modigliani began to tone down his palette, applying the colors in an increasingly realistic manner. This newfound chromatic moderation, however, did not affect his portrayal of stylized forms.

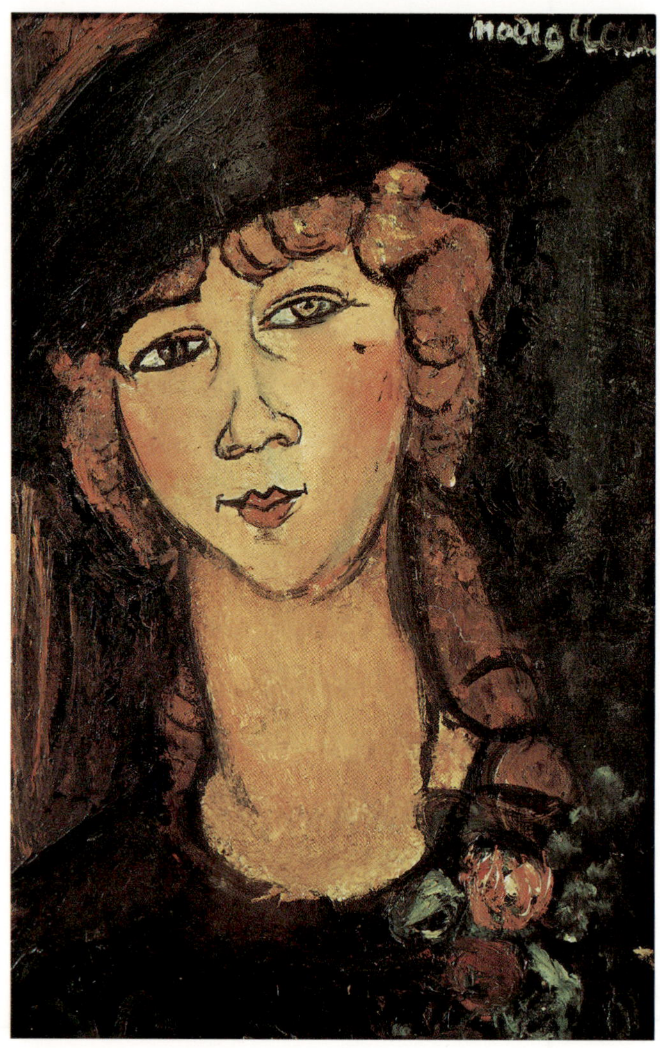

HEAD OF A WOMAN IN A HAT
(LOLOTTE), *c.* 1916.
The lighthearted gaiety
permeating this portrait
is quite exceptional in
Modigliani's production.
This Parisian prostitute
—possibly one of many who fell
for the handsome Amedeo—is,
with her lively, amused eyes,
her flared nostrils, and the
sneer through her makeup,
incompatible with the elusive,
melancholic air that tinges
most of his portraits.

HEAD OF A WOMAN WITH EARRINGS,
1917. The distortion evident
in Modigliani's figures is less
suited to the vulgar charm of
Lolotte (above) than to the
languorous air of refinement
emanating from this portrait,
in which the bluish sockets of
the model's eyes and the tiny
bright dots of her earrings
become the focus of the
viewer's attention.

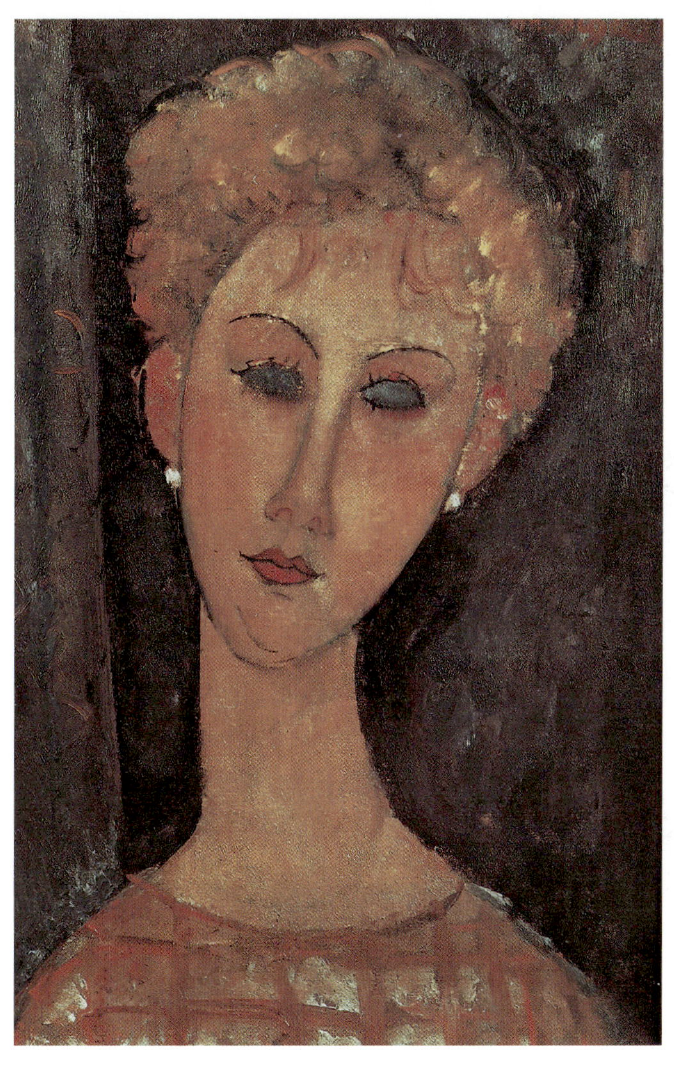

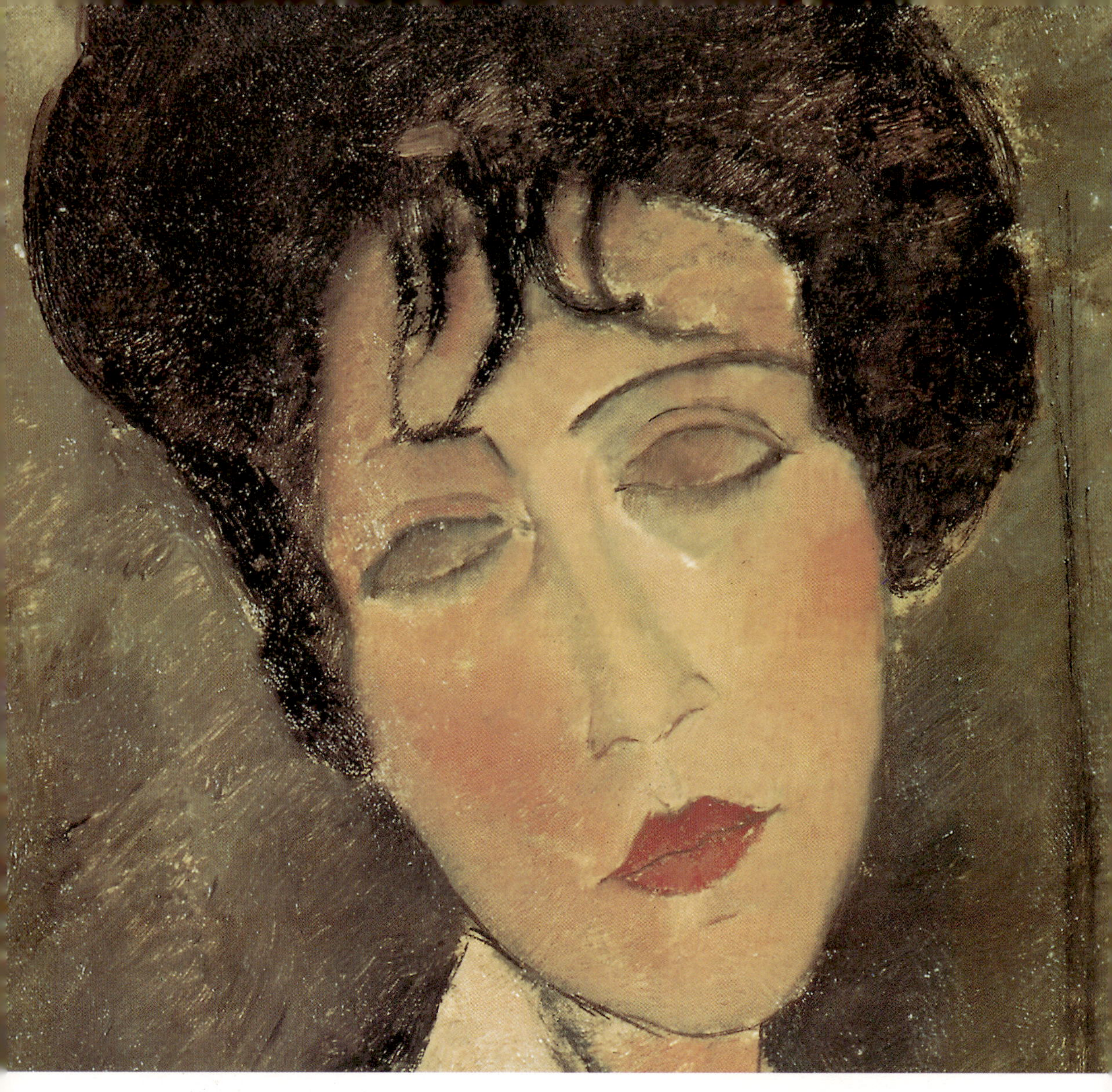

WOMAN IN A BLACK NECKTIE, 1917. Few other works by Modigliani emanate such a mysterious gaze as strongly as this portrait. The artist explained to Léopold Survage that it was an intensely introspective gaze, one similar to those found in images of the pharaoh Akhenaton or in the Charioteer of Delphi, which so fascinated Modigliani. This effect in painting—achieved in sculpture more readily by the character of the materials—enhances the model's remoteness, inviting the viewer to ponder the viability of communication between human beings. The same question is at the foundation of the metaphysical painting of Giorgio de Chirico, another Italian artist.

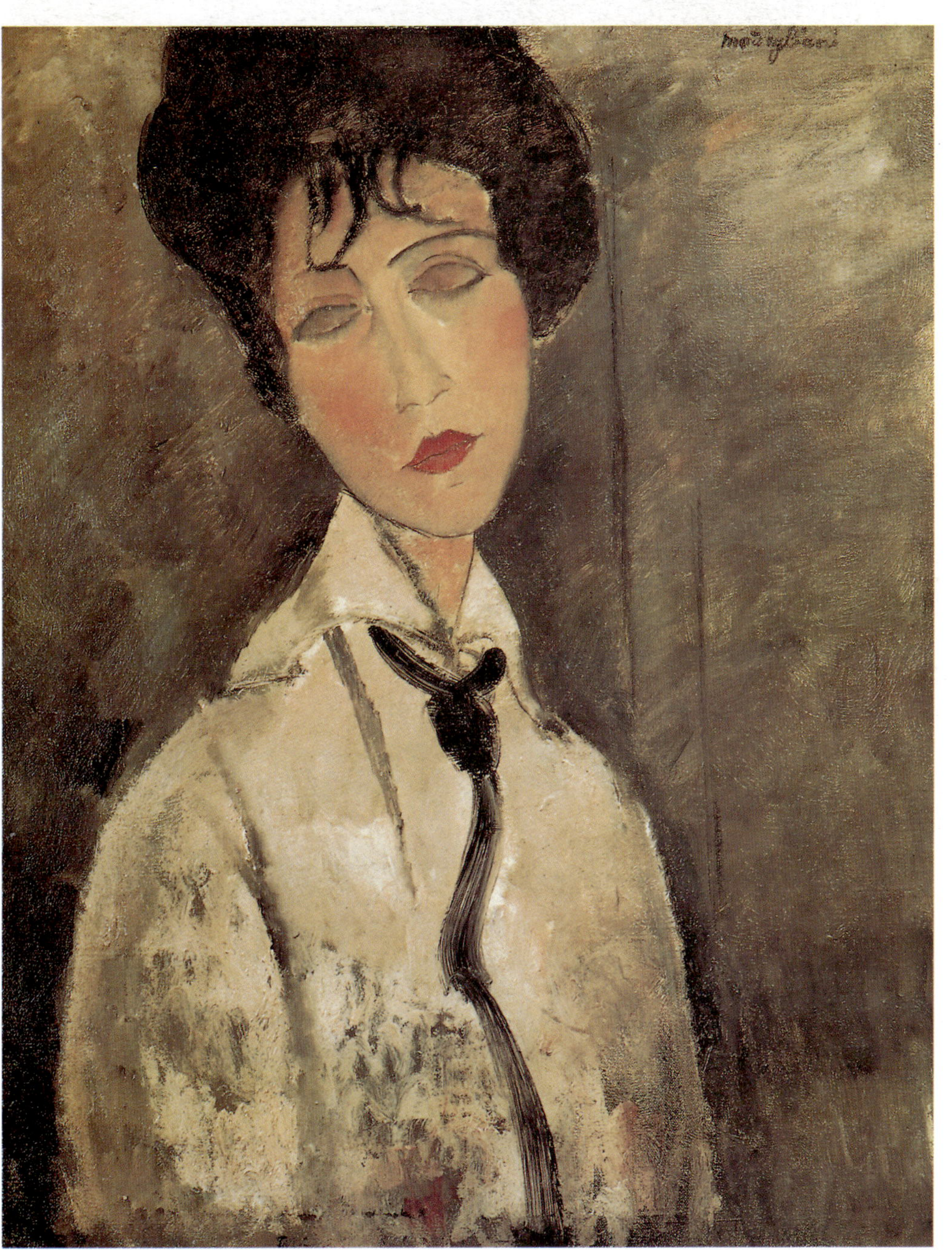

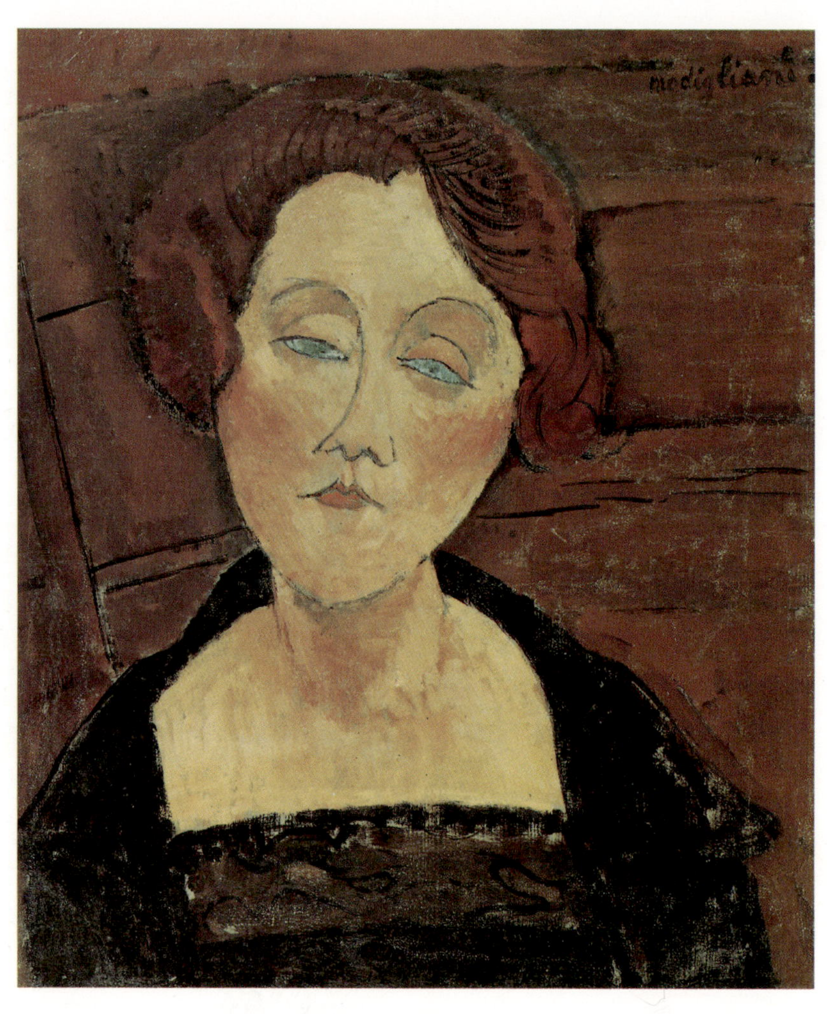

modigliani

WOMAN WITH RED HAIR AND BLUE
EYES, 1917. Modigliani was
partial to auburn hair and
blue eyes, two traits shared by
several of his models, including
Jeanne Hébuterne and the sitter
of this portrait. Here again
the viewer's focus is drawn
to the eyes, who serene blue
color fills their entire surface.
Thanks to his exceptional
draftsmanship, the artist
was able, with only a few
strokes, to imbue the sitter's
countenance with great
expressivness.

SEATED WOMAN (DÉDIE HAYDEN),
1918. This portrait of the wife
of Henry Hayden—a Polish Cubist
painter also residing in Paris
in those years—is evidence of
Modigliani's dependence on a
truthful perception of his
models, which prevented him
from painting them from memory.

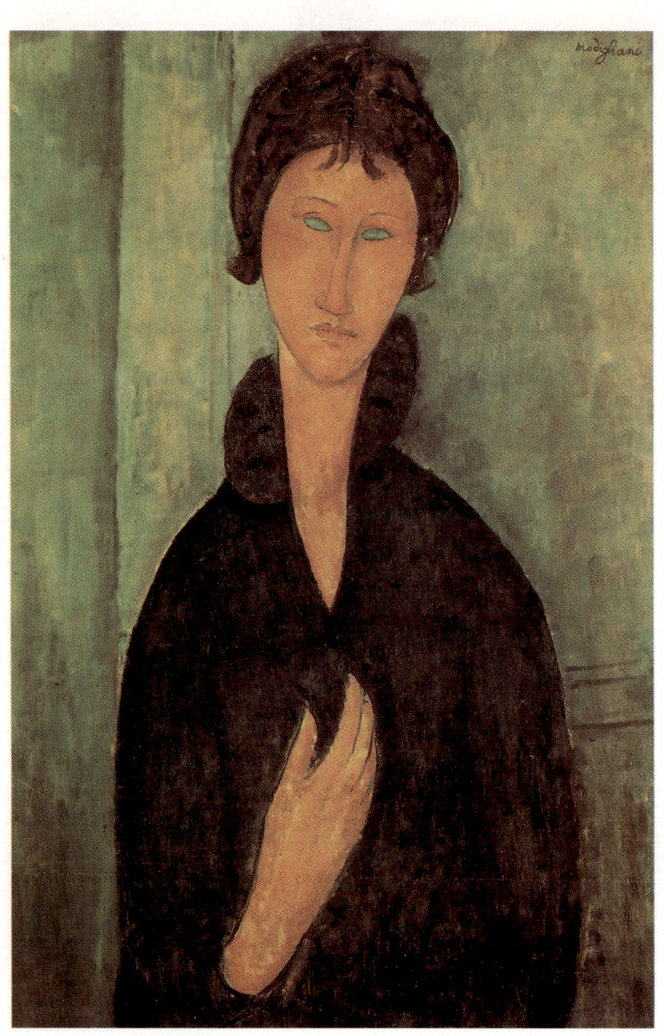

WOMAN WITH BLUE EYES, 1918;
YOUNG GIRL WITH BROWN HAIR,
1918. The neutral backgrounds of
these two portraits underscores
the tactile value of the
sitters' faces. While the
art of this period was
increasingly dominated by
analytic approaches,
Modigliani, in keeping with
his own traditional view of the
painter's role, remained more
concerned with the specifically
tangible aspects of art.

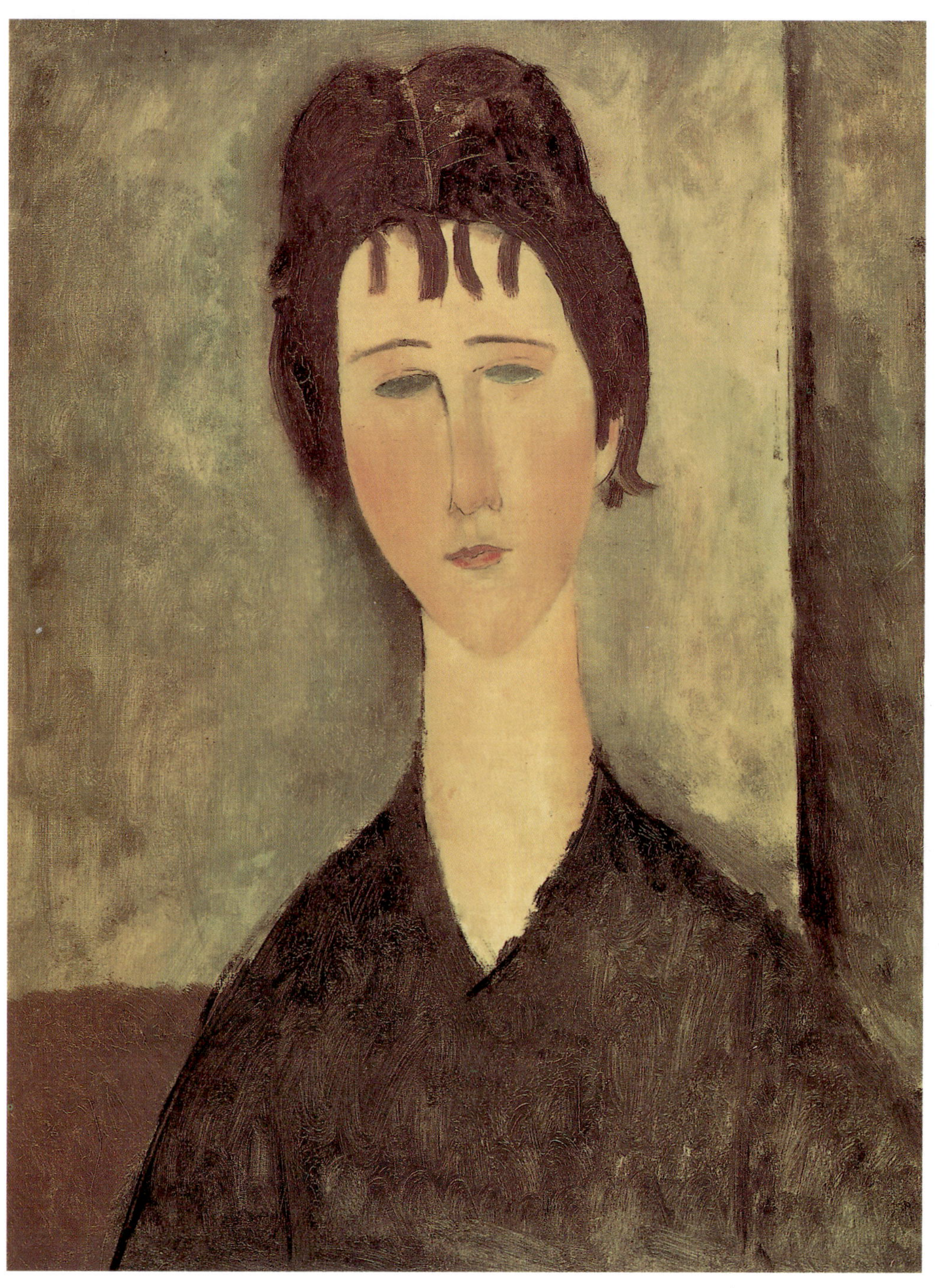

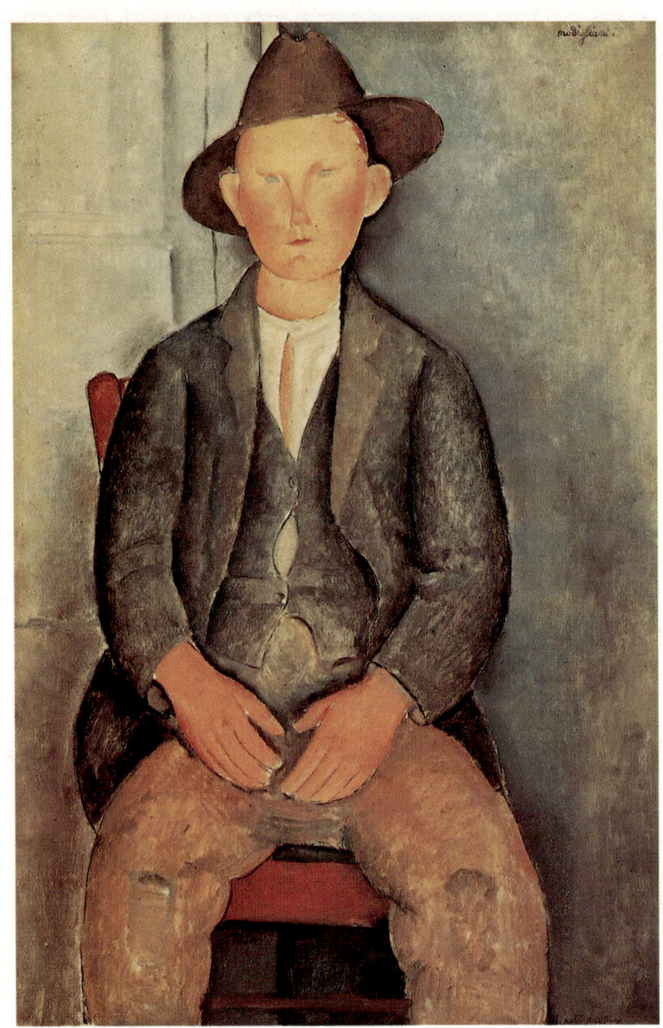

THE LITTLE PEASANT, 1918; YOUNG
PEASANT LEANING AGAINST A TABLE,
1918. Modigliani's portraits
of children, such as the two
shown her, are suffused with
a certain sense of timidity
and defenselessness, perhaps
foreshadowing the melancholy
that tinges the artist's
portrayal of the later stages
of life. The models were
generally young apprentice
workers, whom the hardships of
labor had prematurely forced
into adulthood.

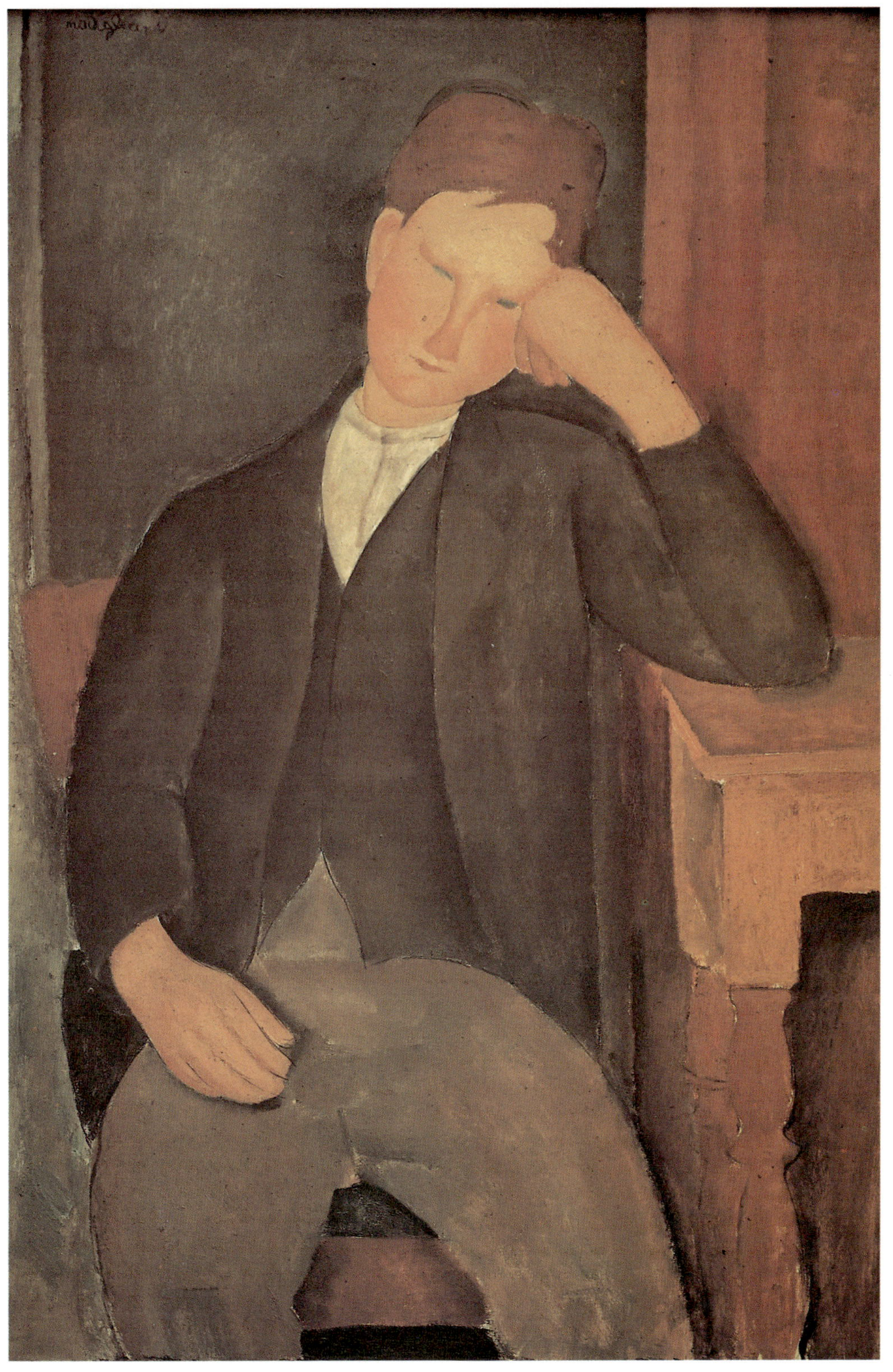

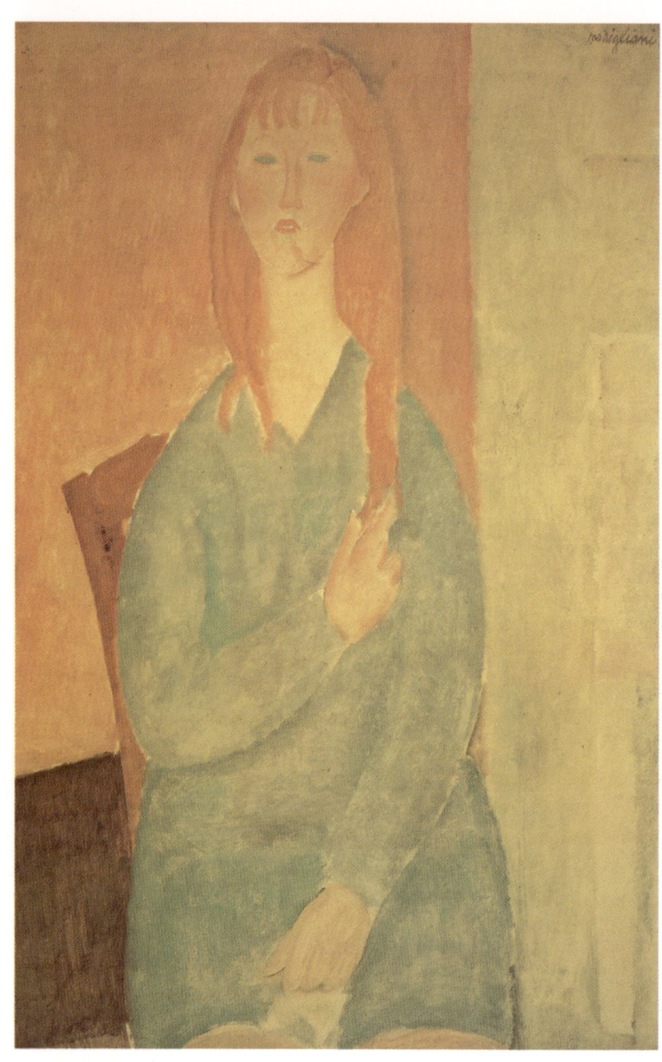

SEATED YOUNG WOMAN WITH LOOSE
HAIR, 1919. In this work,
the painter relinquished his
traditional use of black
strokes to define the figure's
essential lines, opting instead
to construct the image out
of large fields of color.
The painting carefully
avoids all suggestion of
three-dimensionality, as was
characteristic of Modigliani's
lack of interest in spatial
effects.

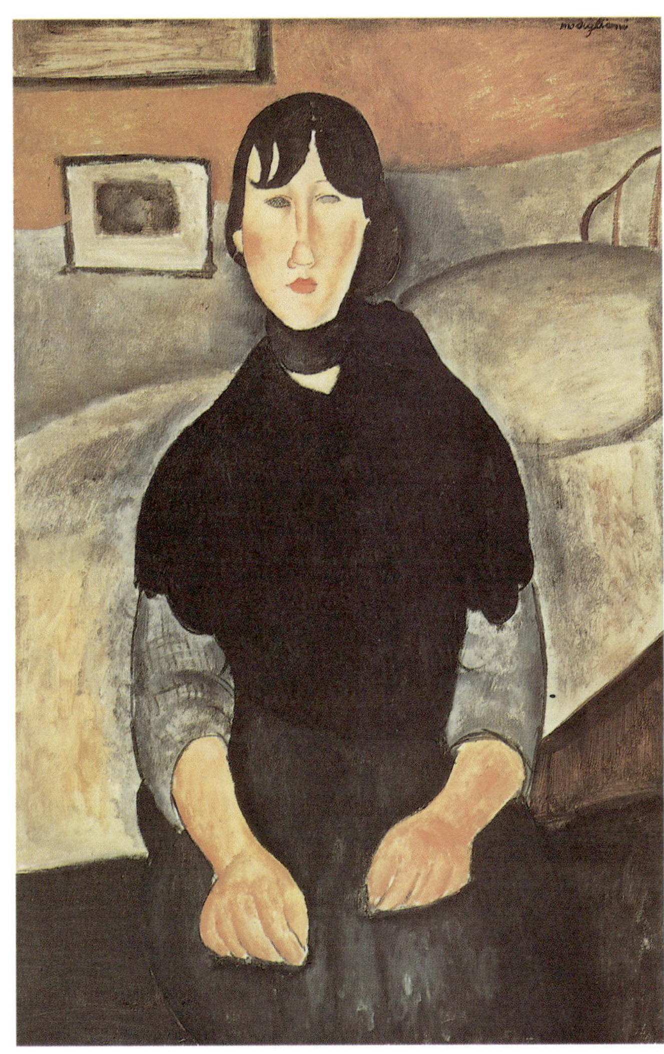

THE COUNTRY GIRL, 1919. The
model of this painting appears
to be Germaine Lable, the
daughter of the concierge of
the building where Modigliani's
friend, the poet Max Jacob,
lived. The young woman is
depicted seated against a
shallow, nearly abstract
background in which the curved
lines of the bed are echoed
by the sinuous contour of
the wainscoting. The overall
seediness of the scene is
brightened somewhat by the
girl's lively beauty and hardy
laborer's hands.

NUDES

Around 1916 Modigliani renewed his interest in nudes—a subject he had already addressed as a sculptor—and a year later his production was consumed by them. While early on his nudes had been characterized by the rigid stylization typical of African statuary, now they concentrated on genuine displays of sensuality. Unlike his portraits, the faces of these nudes are rendered with just a few simple lines. This shifts the focus of the painting onto the sitter's body, which is modeled by a combination of a sinuous contour traced in dense black strokes and impasto brushwork, producing a strong tactile sensation. Modigliani's distinctive framing of these nudes crops the figure at midthigh, causing the rest of the sensuous body to flood the canvas. Sometimes the model is portrayed in the pose of a "modest Venus," but more often the figure exudes a quiet shamelessness that is also highly erotic. This quality did not go unnoticed by the Parisian police, who ordered the removal of some of the nudes exhibited at Modigliani's first and only ore-man show at the Berthe Weill gallery in December 1917. Not just the vivid representation of the models' pubic hair upset the zealous functionaries; they were presumably also outraged by the immorality of the tranquil display of a naked body without an allegorical reference or formal euphemism. Edouard Manet achieved similarly scandalous results a few decades earlier with his *Olympia*.

SEATED NUDE, 1916. This was the first in the series of nudes that characterized Modigliani's output in the years 1916 and 1917. While the use of lines continues to be essential in the artist's work, especially in tracing the figure's contour and in drawing the features of the model's face, these images appear to possess a new quality: a sensuality that is more empathetic in nature, as expressed by the painter's choice of a warmer palette in which the prevailing orange and rose hues occasionally give way to ravishing dashes of violet.

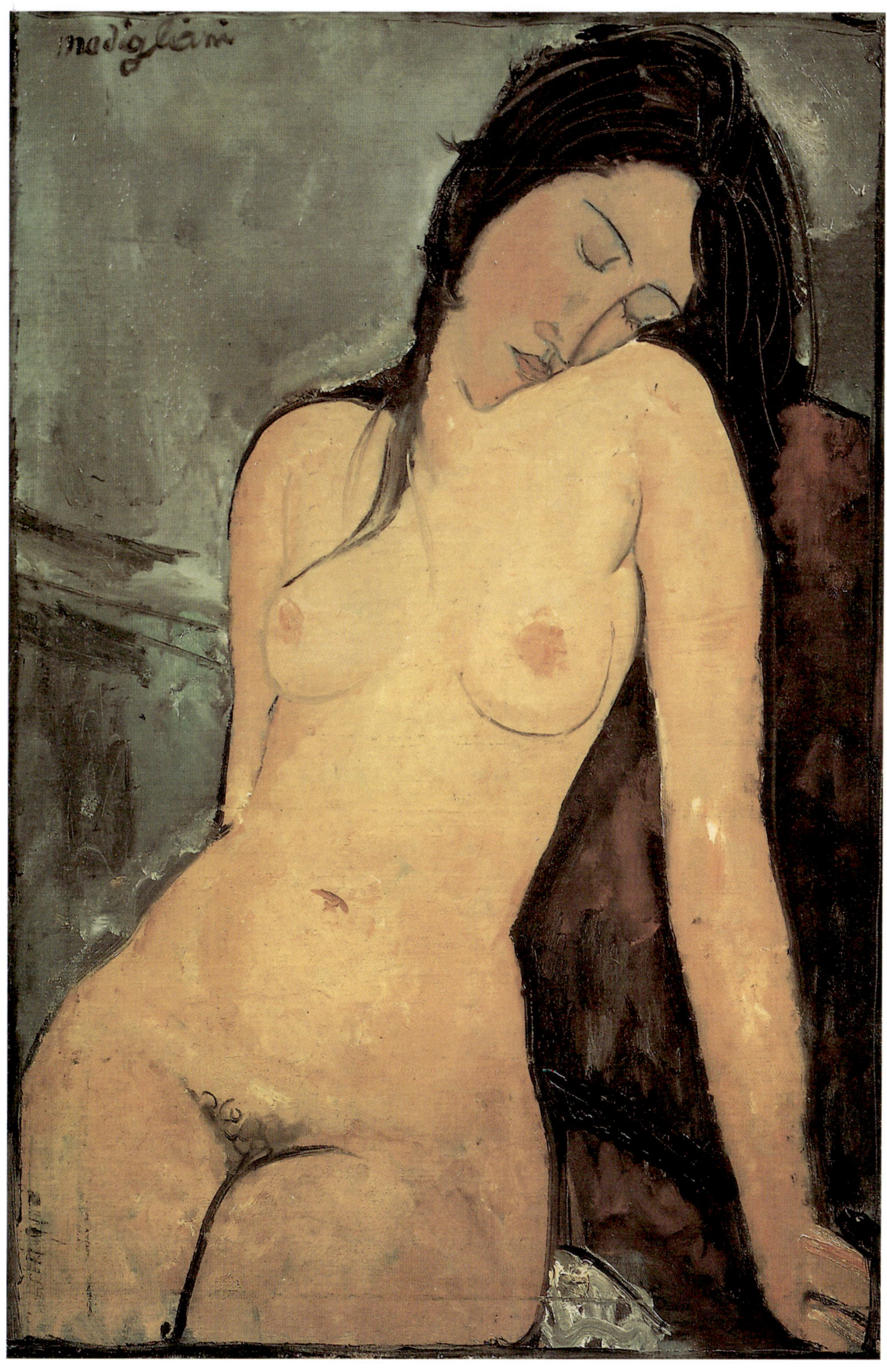

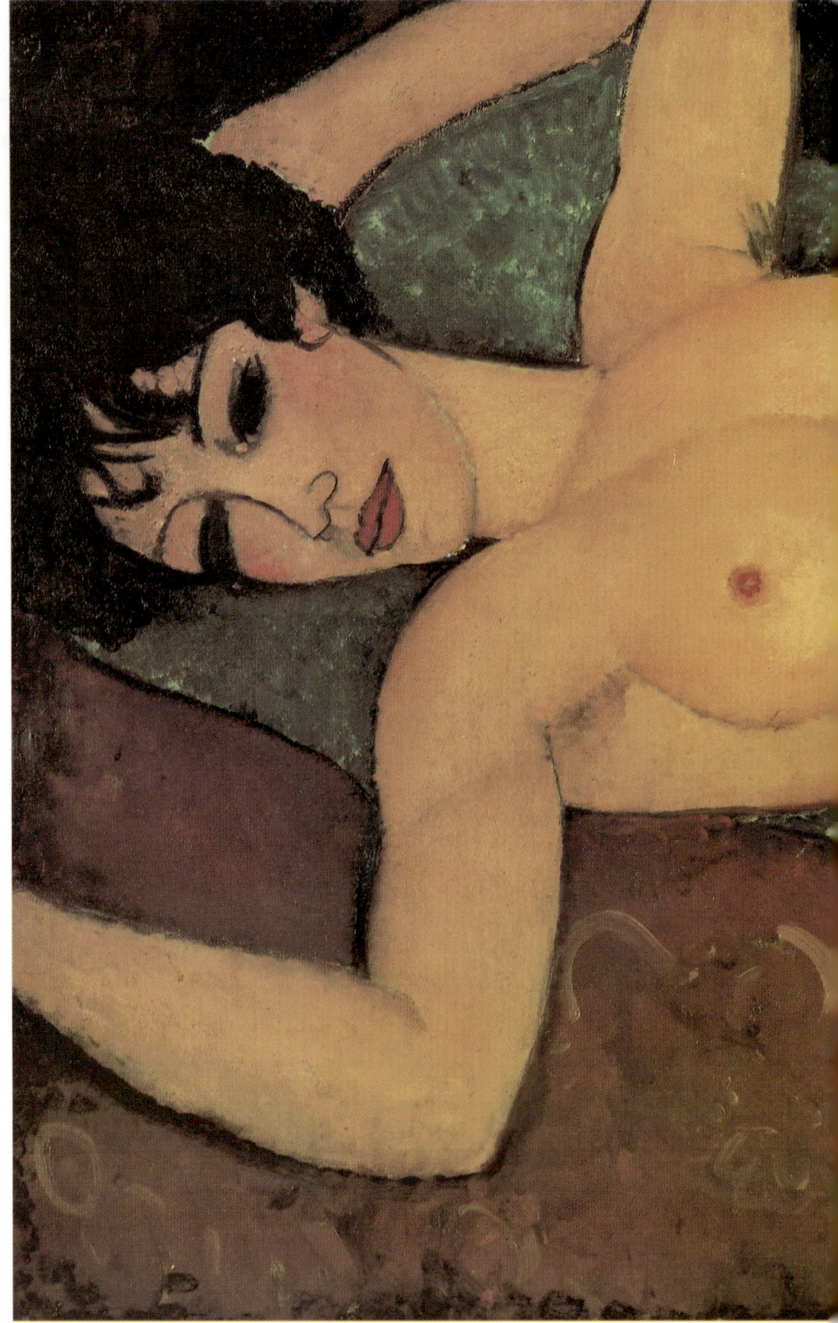

NUDE ON A CUSHION, 1917.
Having left behind the stylized
rigidity of his sculptural
phase, Modigliani revels here
in the opulence of the woman's
splendid figure, inviting the
viewer to gaze on her almost
voyeuristically. To emphasize
this effect, he has framed
the image in a peculiarly
fragmentary way, not just
cropping the figure midthigh
—a characteristic feature of
Modigliani's nudes—but also
leaving out portions of
the arms and head entirely.
The body is modeled with a
painstaking, subtle brushwork
that lingers over a wide range
of warm tonalities, completely
in contrast to the abstract
nature of the bed of pillows,
rendered in thick palpable
strokes. The end result is a
contemplative, pacified nude
woman, much in keeping with
the grand tradition of Titian
and Velázquez.

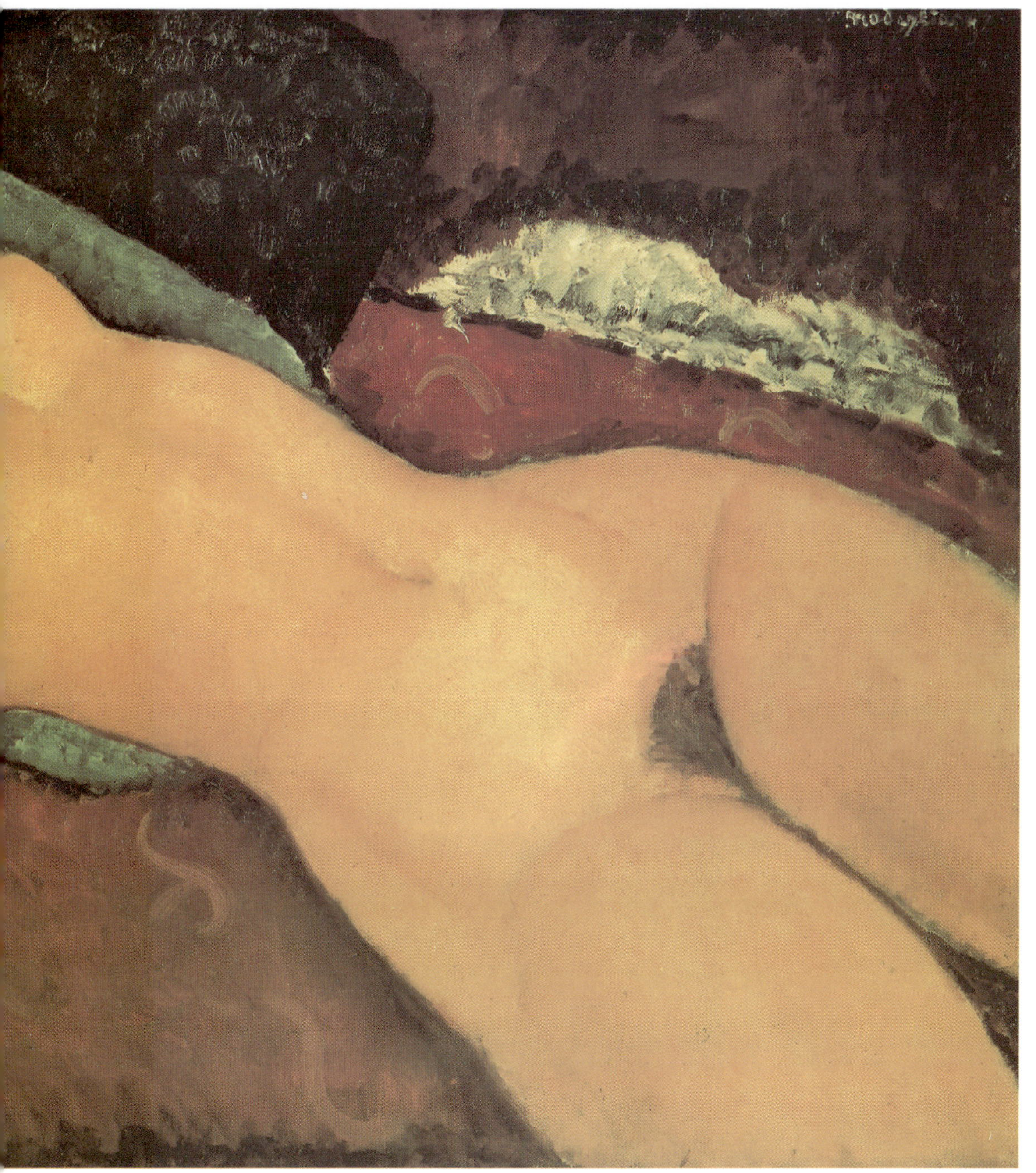

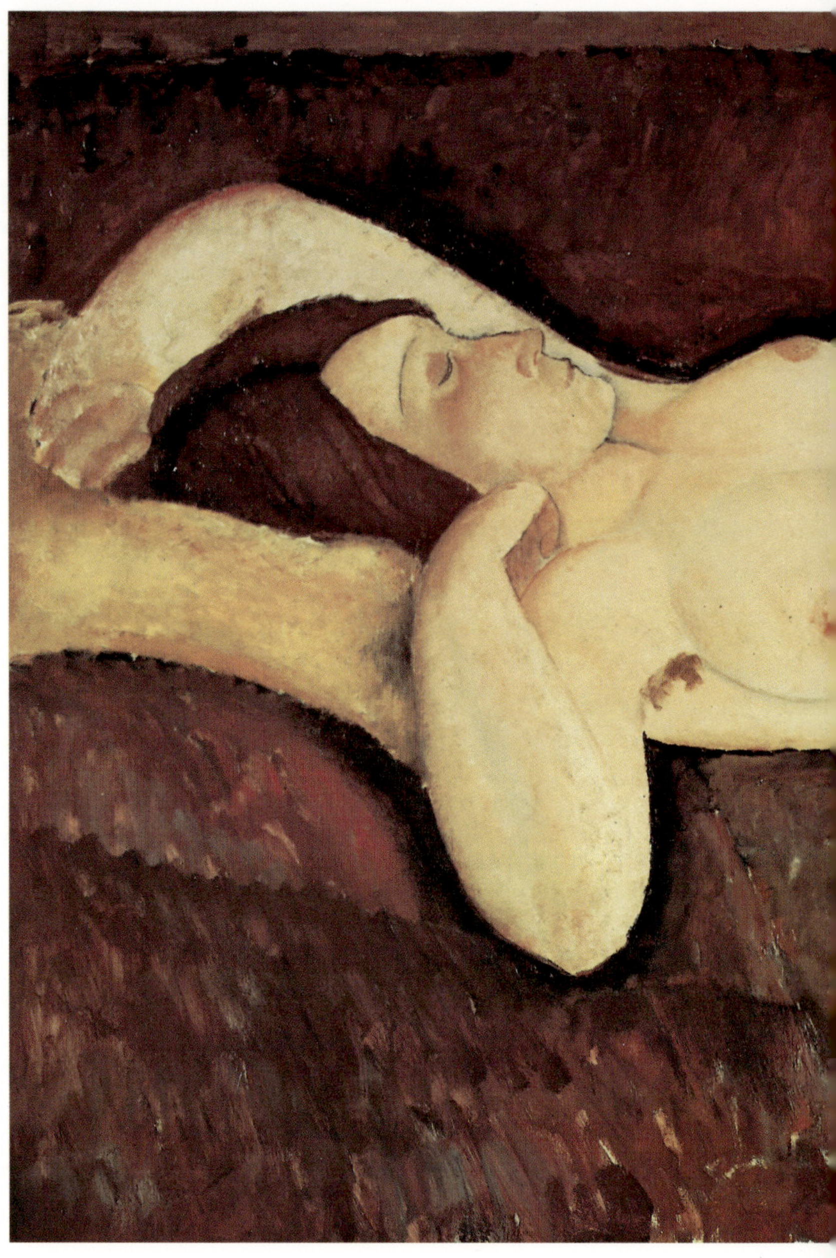

RECLINING NUDE (LE GRAND NU), 1917. In time, Modigliani's nudes became increasingly delicate, losing the solid black outlines and fiery orange hues in favor of a softer harmony of pale tones that melt directly into a background still constructed out of broad brushstrokes. Modigliani thus established himself as one of the great masters of the nude painting, inspiring one of his first patrons, Francis Carco, to state in 1919, "The sometimes soft, animal-like stillness, with its erotic abandon and subtle contentment, have never before found a painter so eager to depict this."

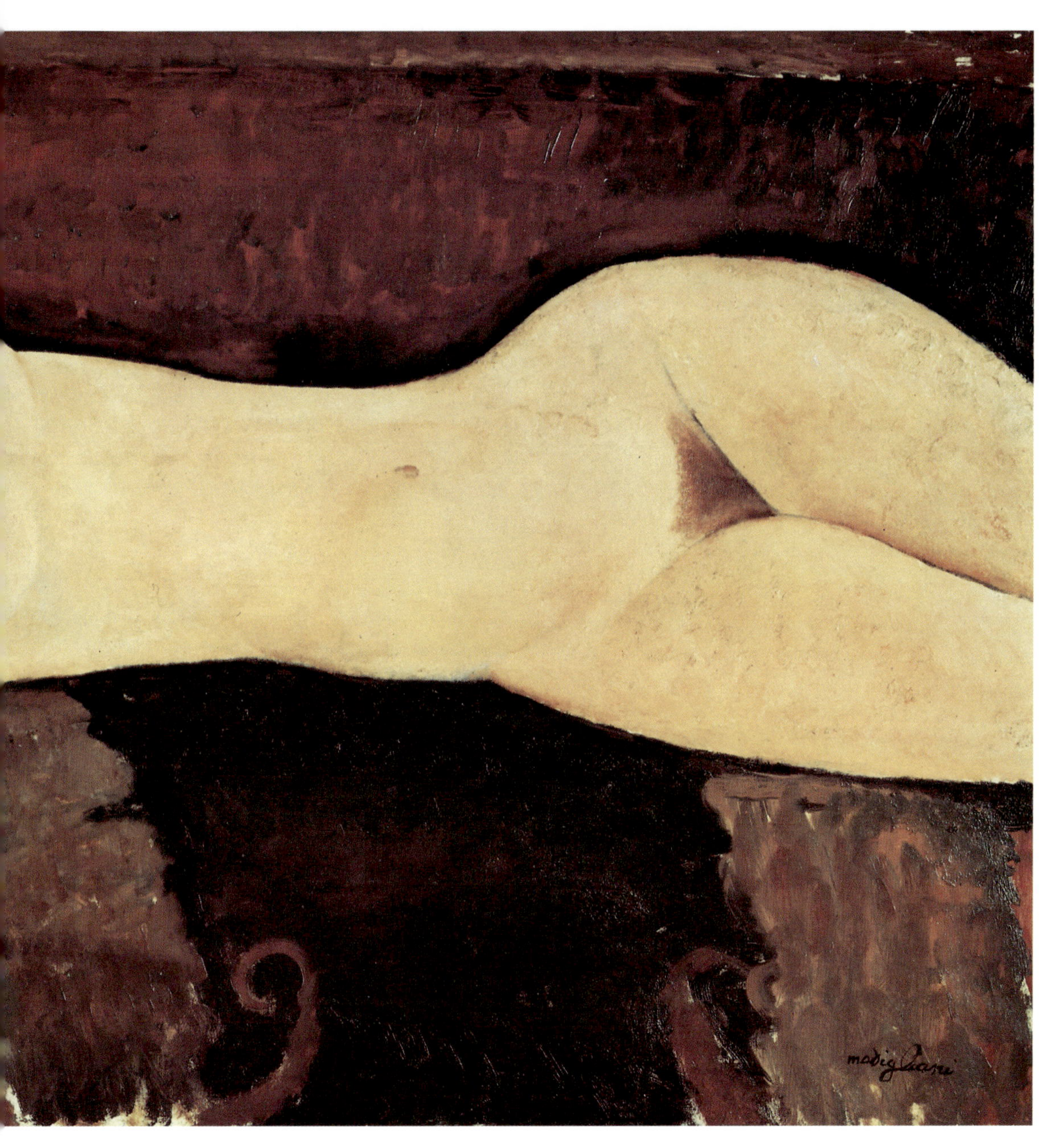

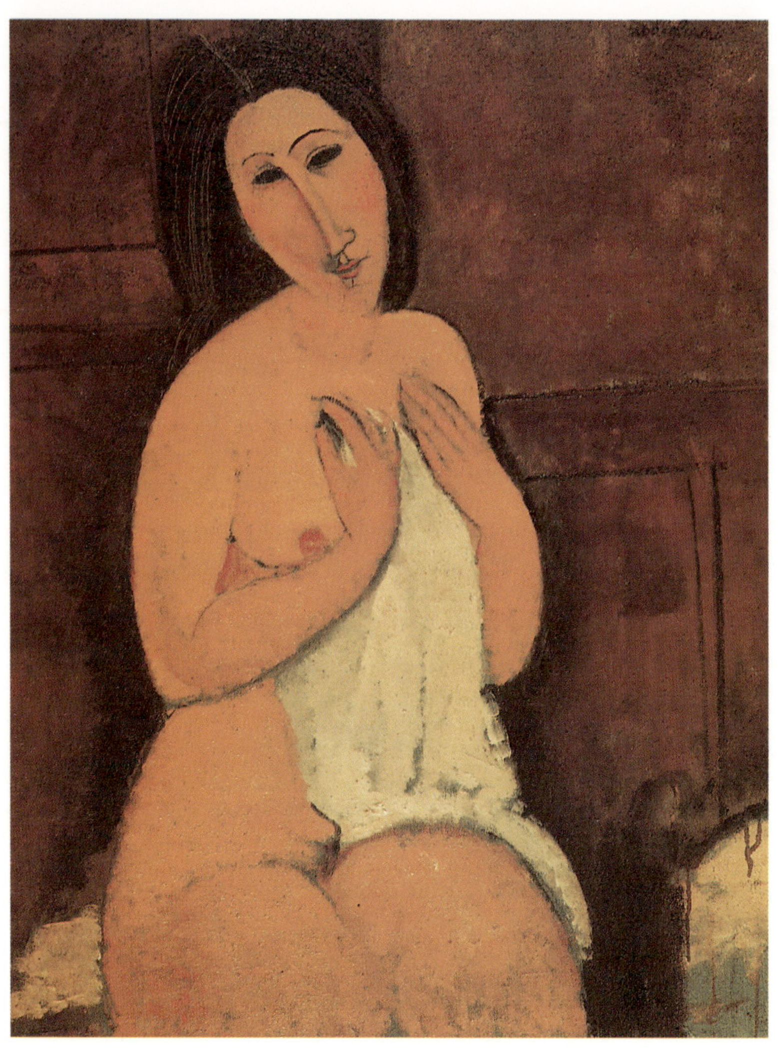

SEATED NUDE WITH A SHIRT IN HER HANDS, 1917. While Modigliani's reclining nudes display a certain lax indifference, those that are seated exude a more withdrawn attitude, at once modest and somewhat helpless. Modigliani's method did not treat the pictorial surface consistently throughout, so the painstaking application of thick brushwork to flesh contrasts clearly with the more hurried treatment of the hair, which becomes a large black patch, scratched when the paint was still fresh to let the primer show through.

THE PARISIAN BOHEMIA

Modigliani's inability to pay for models, together with the lack of
clients during the harsh years of World War I—when he was finally
beginning to gain recognition—explain why the artist's works are
populated almost exclusively by men, women, and children from his
own circle, most of whom belonged to the artistic bohemia of Paris.
Jean Cocteau, one of the painter's acquaintances, aptly described
this scene when he said that "in Montparnasse we could afford
the luxury of being poor; poverty was fun." Modigliani portrayed
each of his fellow bohemians in turn, including Chaïm Soutine, a
Lithuanian-born Jew who was destitute but had boundless admiration
for the Italian artist; Beatrice Hastings, a writer who worked for a
British magazine and had a tempestuous love affair with Modigliani;
the poet Leopold Zborowski and his wife Hanka, who started out
as commercial advisors to Modigliani and eventually became his
caretakers when he fell ill; and, above all, Jeanne Hébuterne,
the artist's last great love, who gave up everyting to follow her
unstable—and occasionally unfaithful—companion even into death.
The relationship that bound all of these figures to Modigliani was
summed up in a tribute by the poet Max Jacob: "Like an aristocrat,
you led a life of simple grandeur. We love you."

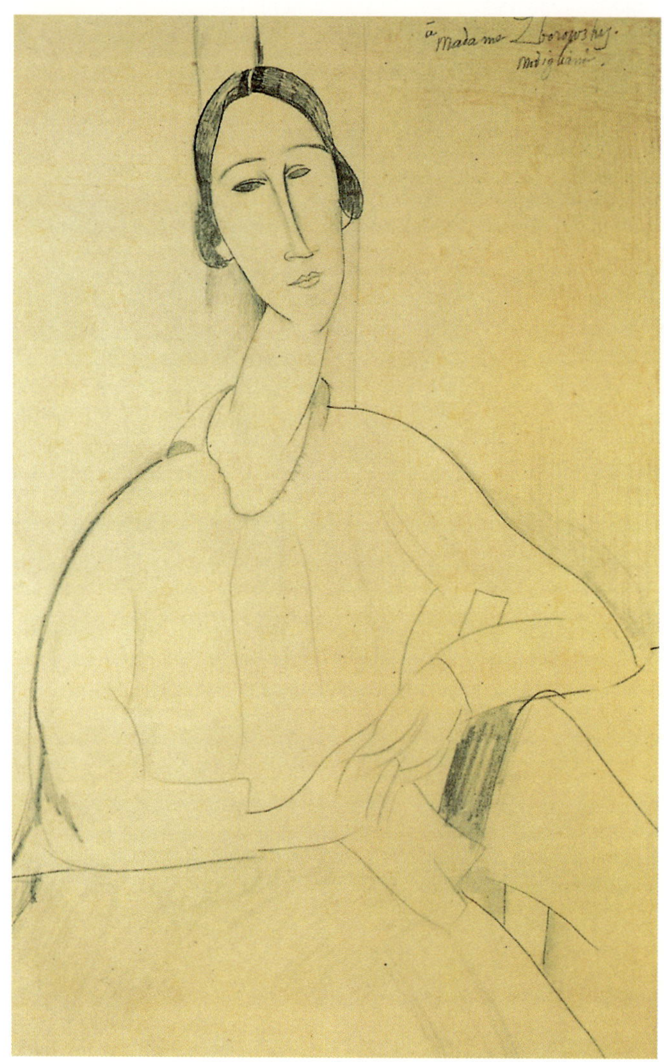

PORTRAIT OF HANKA ZBOROWSKA, *c.* 1917; PORTRAIT OF ARISTIDE SOMMAT, *c.* 1918. These two portraits are evidence of Modigliani's excellent draftsmanship. While the former is an unhurried figure study and the latter a swift sketch (one of many he executed on the spot to indulge the request of a friend), both drawings show the same measured strokes made with an economy of resources that exhibit Modigliani's extraordinary dexterity.

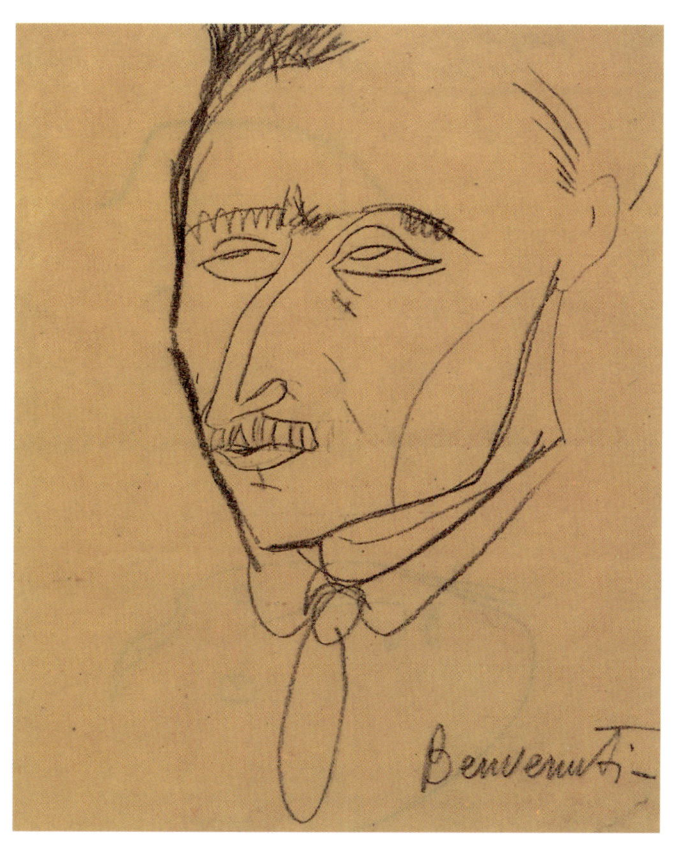

Benvenuti

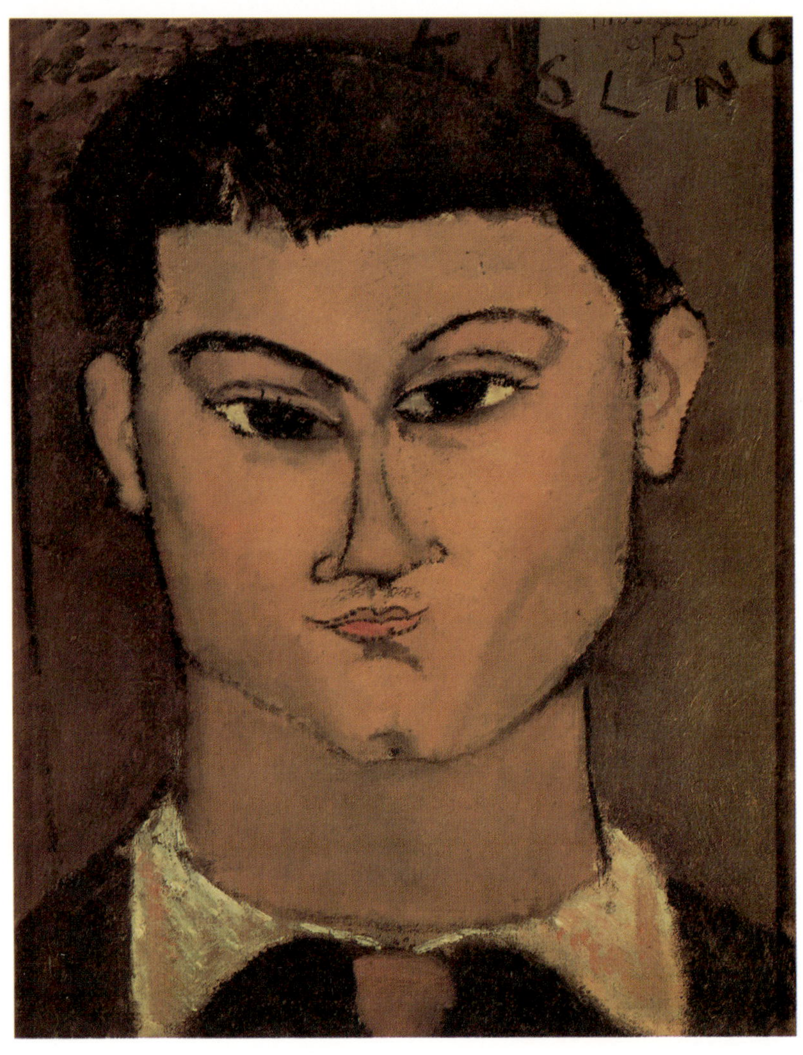

HEAD OF KISLING, 1915. The
Polish-born Moïse Kisling was
one of Modigliani's closest
friends. Both artists were
Jewish, and both had left their
respective countries to live
abroad. An extroverted and
generous painter given to
unbridled, boisterous acts
of revelry, he enjoyed a
recognition that Modigliani
never experienced during his
lifetime. Kisling's liveliness
and joie de vivre are clearly
conveyed in this portrait
by his angular features and
prominent jaw, elements that
also attest the extent to
which Cubist aesthetics were
influencing the work of the
Italian artist in those years.

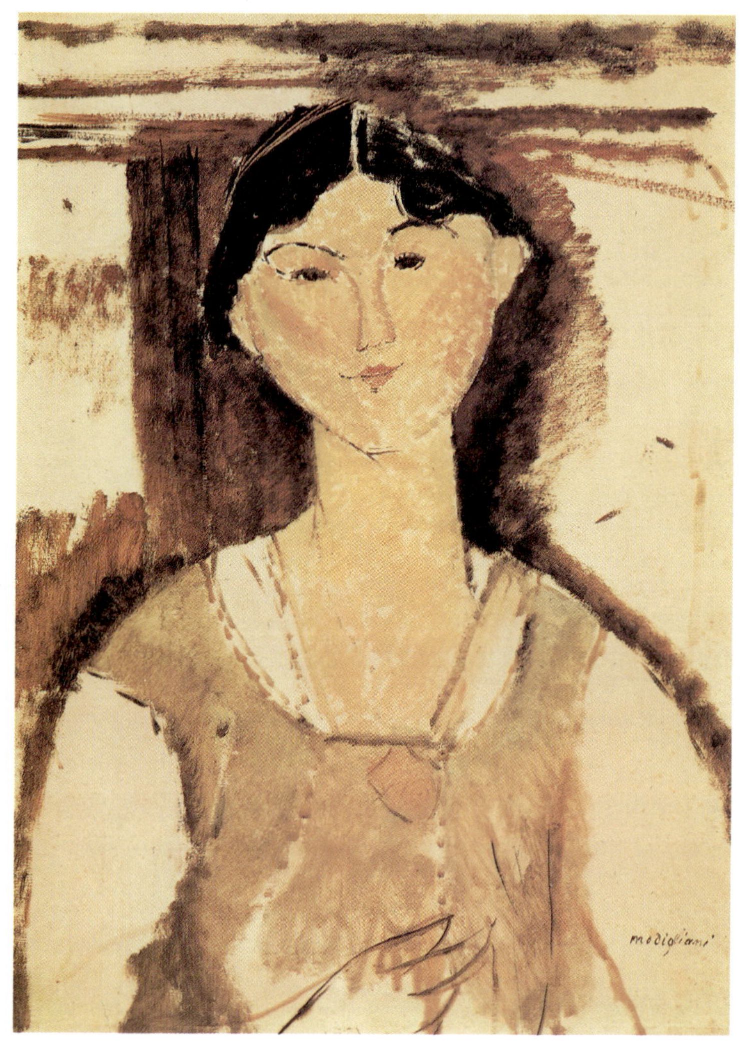

PORTRAIT OF BEATRICE HASTINGS, 1915. This is one of a number of portraits Modigliani made of the South African poet and journalist with whom he had a passionate affair, but the frail, delicate image in no way corresponds to the description of Beatrice given by her contemporaries.

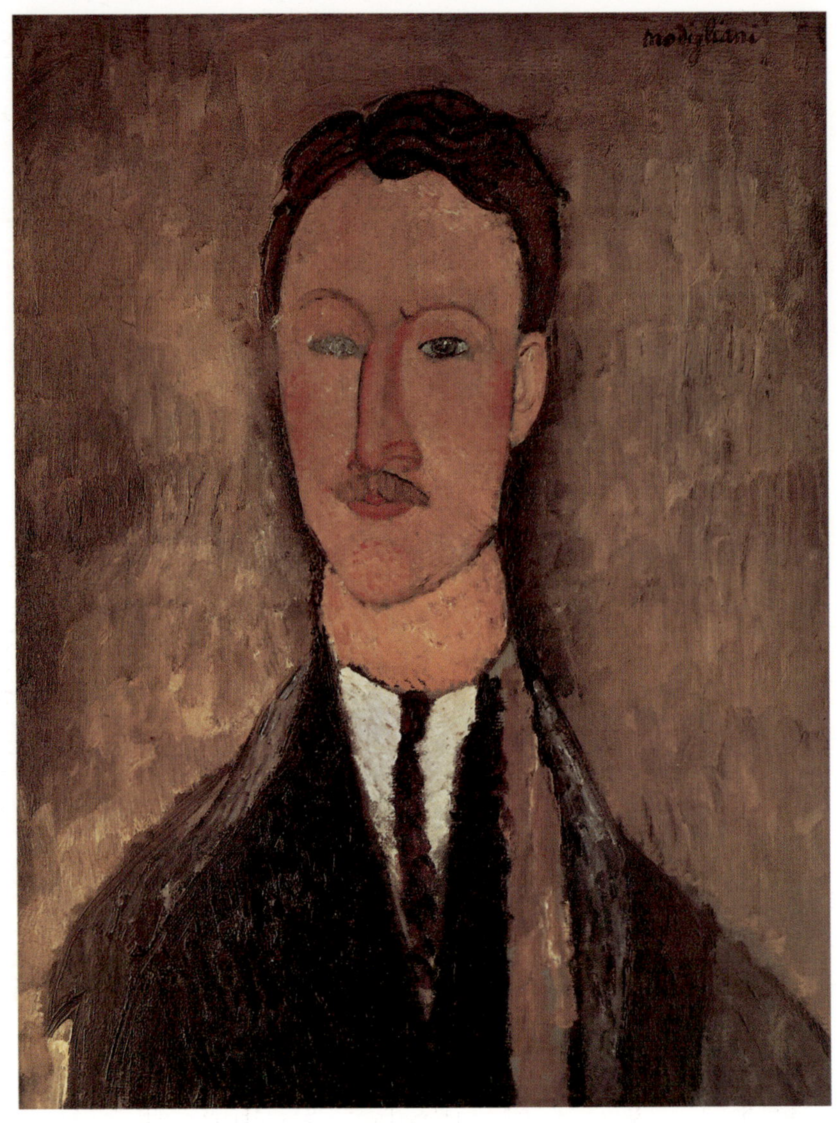

PORTRAIT OF LÉOPOLD SURVAGE, c. 1917. Survage, a painter and set designer with Cubist inclinations, shared both a studio with Modigliani and his alcoholic excesses, especially during their sojourn in Nice in 1918. Modigliani justified giving the sitter only one "normal" eye by explaining, "With one eye you are looking at the outside world, while with the other you are looking within yourself."

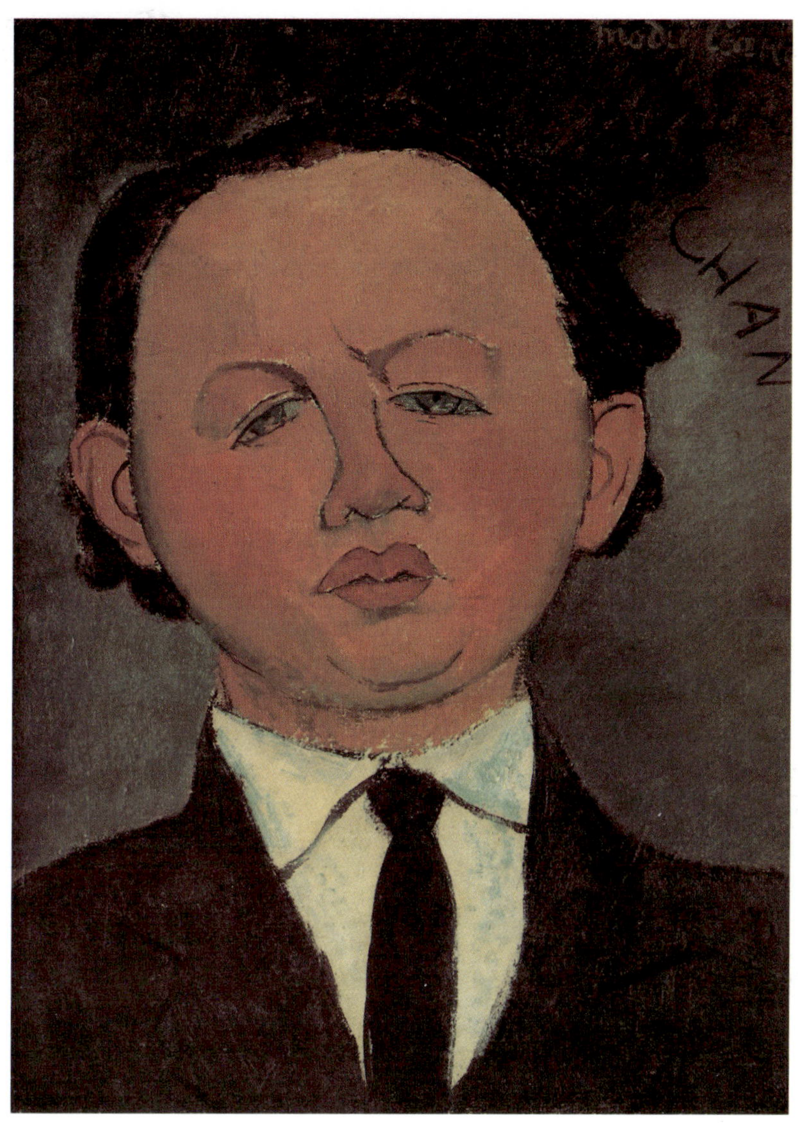

PORTRAIT OF OSCAR MIESTCHANINOFF, "MECHAN", 1917. This sitter is the Russian sculptor Oscar Miestchaninoff, whom the Italian artist familiarly called "Mechan." Unlike the typical elongated figures of Modigliani's other paintings, Miestchaninoff's dull and disgusted expression is inscribed in a nearly perfect circumference.

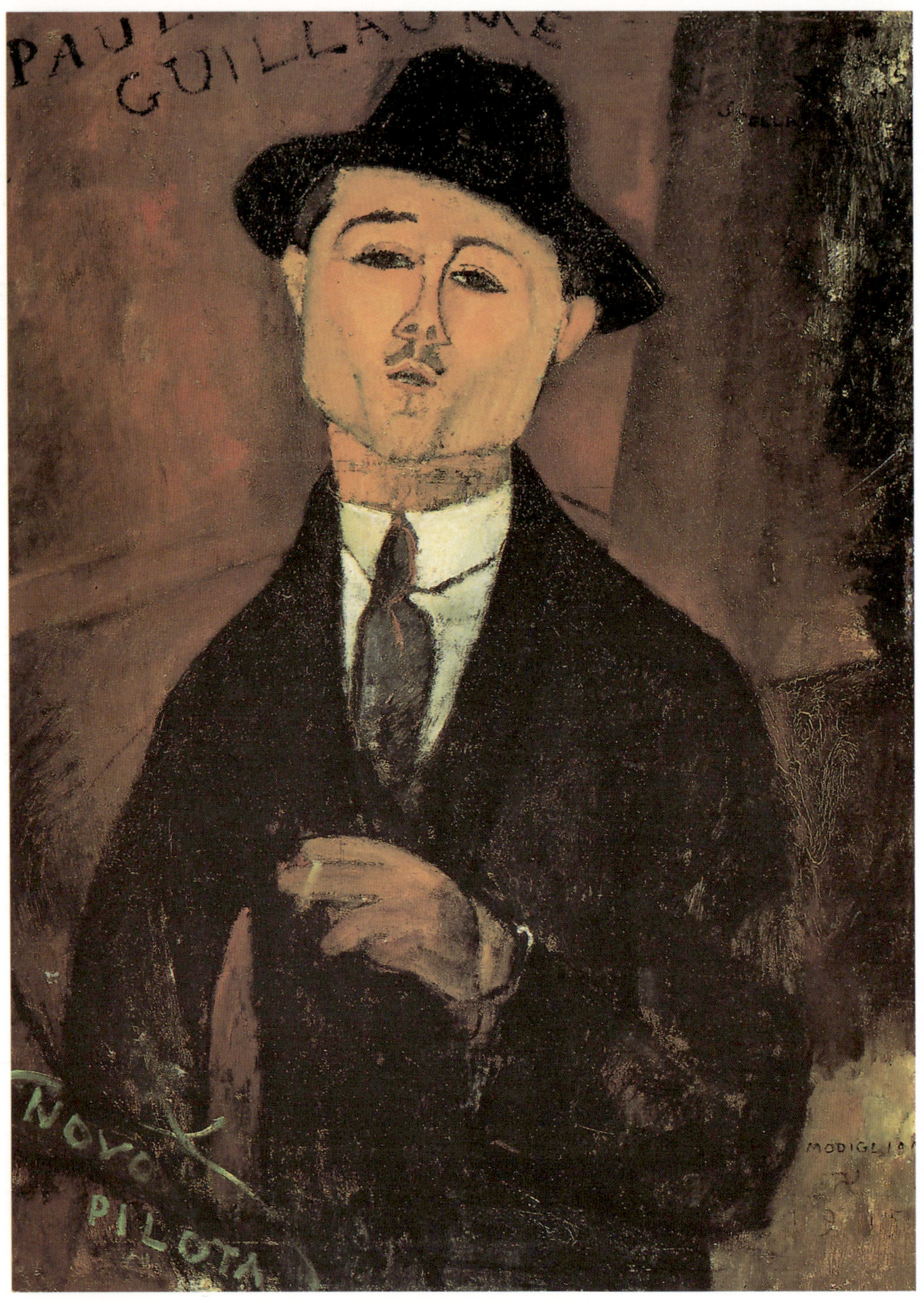
PAUL
GUILLAUME
NOVO
PILOTA

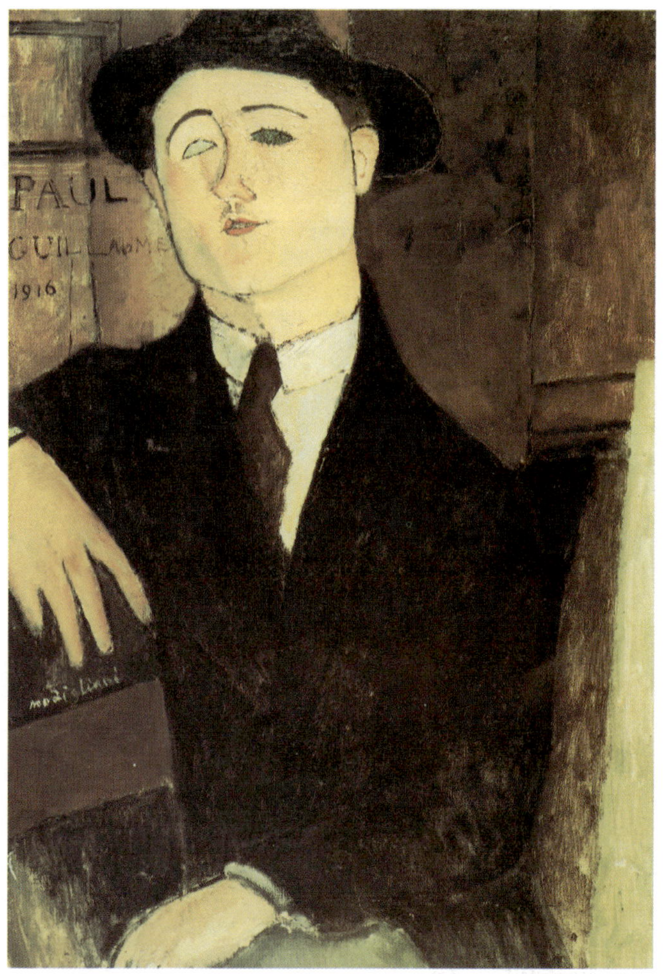

PAUL GUILLAUME, "NOVO PILOTA",
1915; PORTRAIT OF PAUL
GUILLAUME, 1916. Between 1914
and 1917, Guillaume was in
effect virtually the sole
client who held enough trust
and interest in Modigliani
to purchase any of his works.
The angularity of the sitter's
features is characteristic of
the artist's receptiveness to
Cubist influences at this stage.
Two inscriptions in the first
of these portraits—"Stella
Maris" and "Novo Pilota"—are
the painter's homage to his
benefactor, whose role is thus
elevated to leader of an entire
new generation of artists.

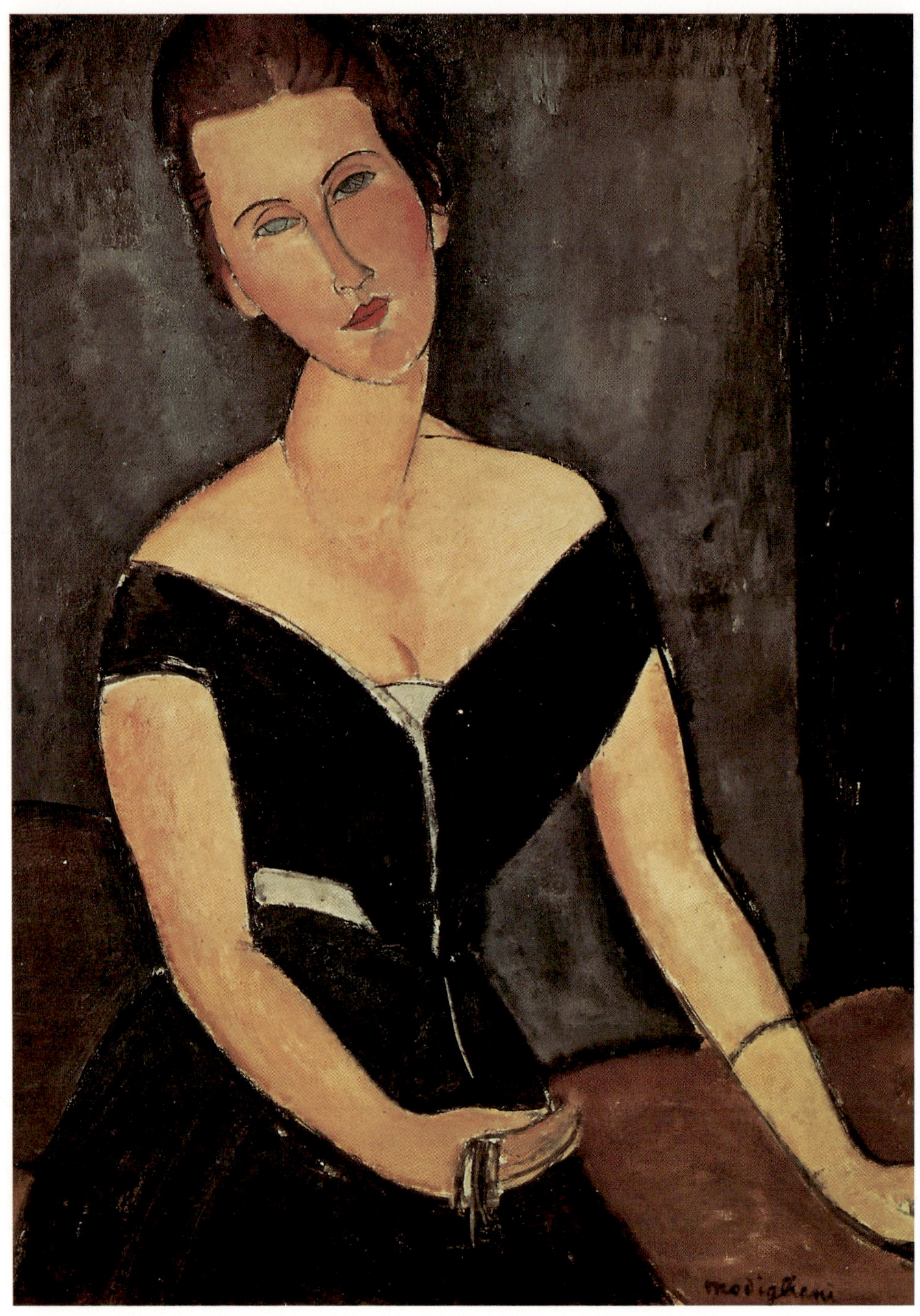

PORTRAIT OF MADAME GEORGES VAN MUYDEN, 1917. This is quite possibly one of a small number of portraits Modigliani painted as a commission, since his models generally belonged to his circle of fellow bohemians. These circumstances account for the more composed, elegant, and self-possessed nature of the sitter.

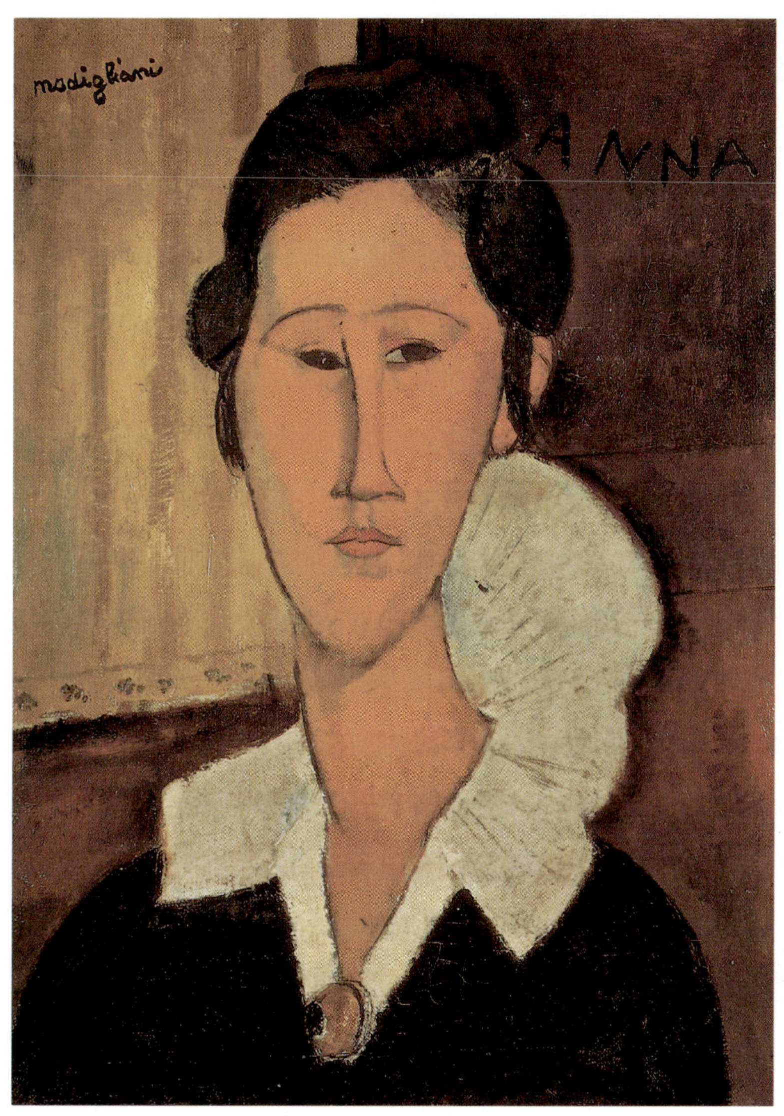

PORTRAIT OF MADAME HANKA ZBOROWSKA, 1917. This is one of the earliest in a long series of portraits that Modigliani painted of the wife of Leopod Zborowski. The Cubist influence is unmistakable in the asymmetrical treatment of the model's features and in the peculiar representation of the fanned-out collar of her blouse.

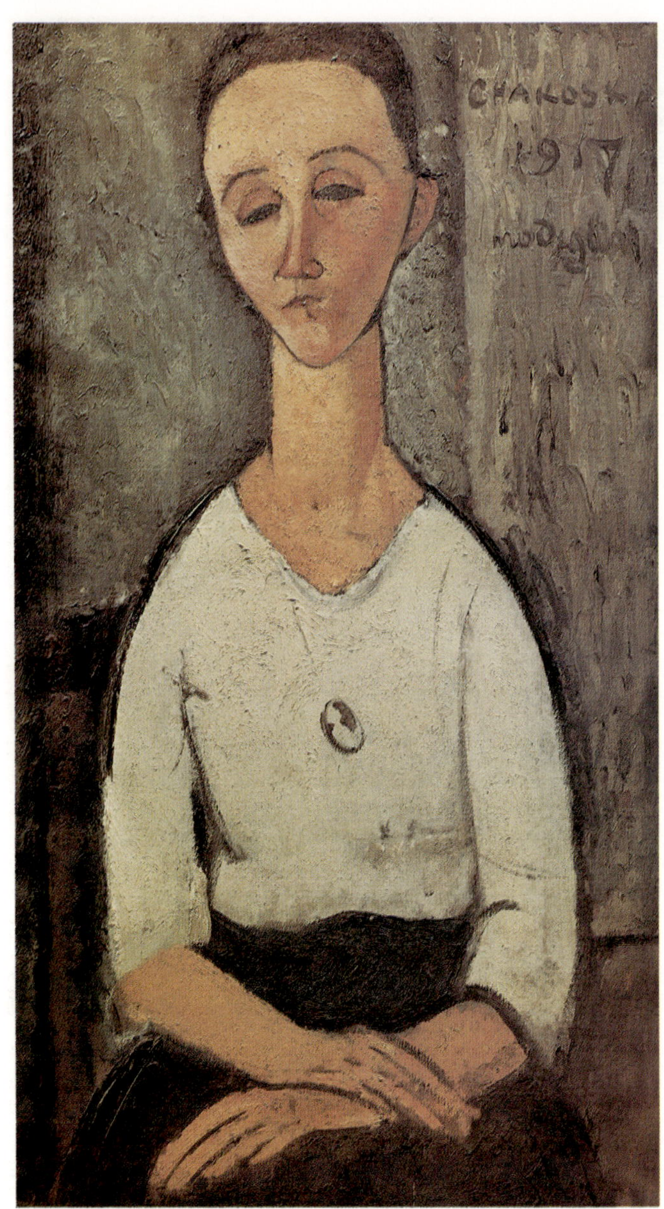

PORTRAIT OF LUNIA CZECHOWSKA, 1917; PORTRAIT OF JEANNE HÉBUTERNE IN A STRAW HAT, 1917. Here are two women of vastly different temperaments whose presence played a crucial role in the artist's final years after his tempestuous involvement with Beatrice Hastings. While Jeanne was the submissive companion, able to endure her lover's excesses, Lunia proved the more mature and experienced woman, ultimately becoming his closest friend and confidante. Her relationship with Modigliani was always of a platonic nature, which is surprising given the painter's promiscuous habite.

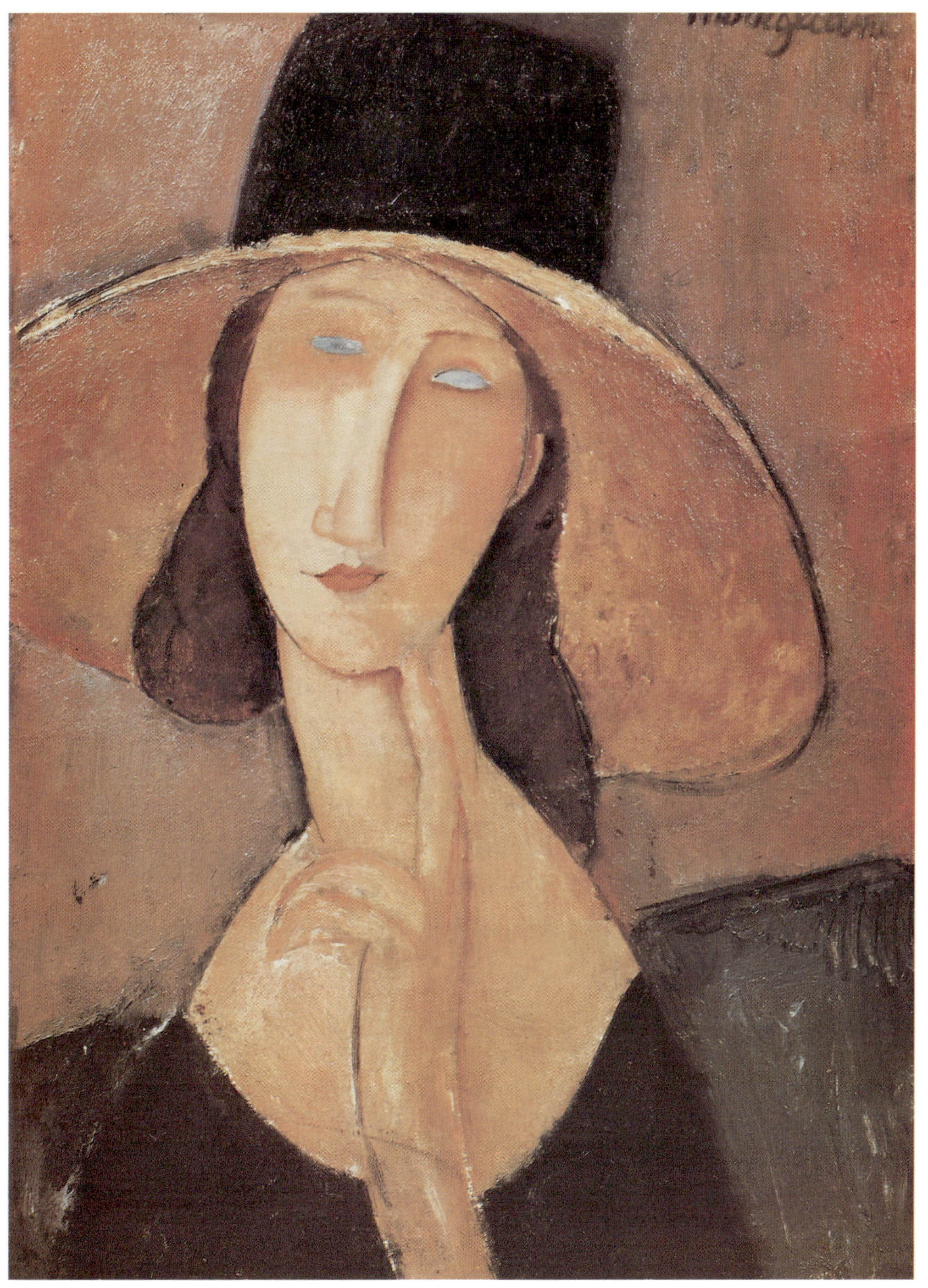

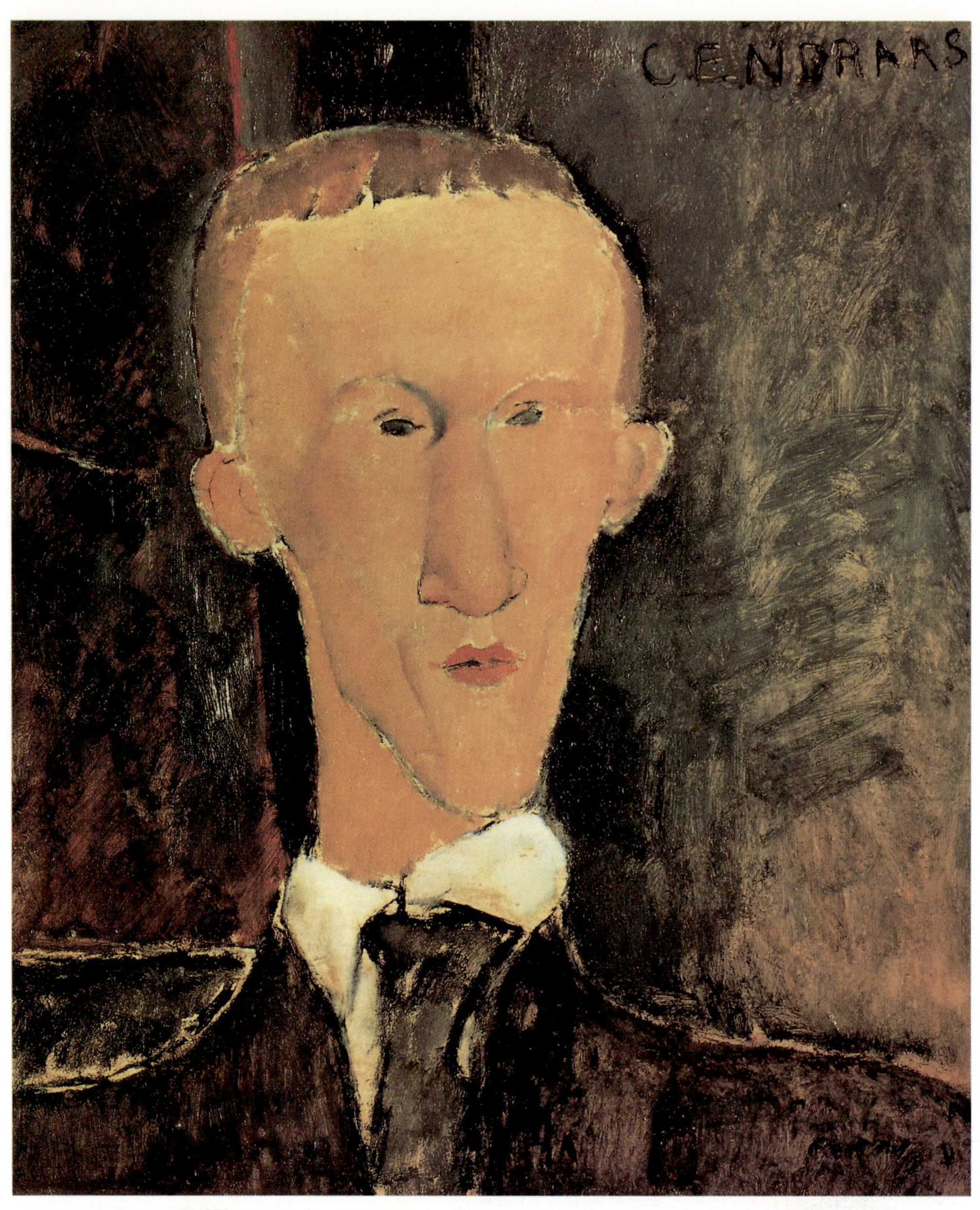

PORTRAIT OF BLAISE CENDRARS, 1917. Modigliani painted this portrait of Cendrars shortly after the latter had returned from the war with a wound that resulted in his arm being amputated. On the occasion of the exhibition of the painter's works at the Berthe Weill gallery in 1917, Cendrars wrote an introductory text entitled "On a Portrait by Modigliani: The Inner World / The Human Heart with / Its 17 Movements / In the Spirit /And the Ups and Downs of Passion."

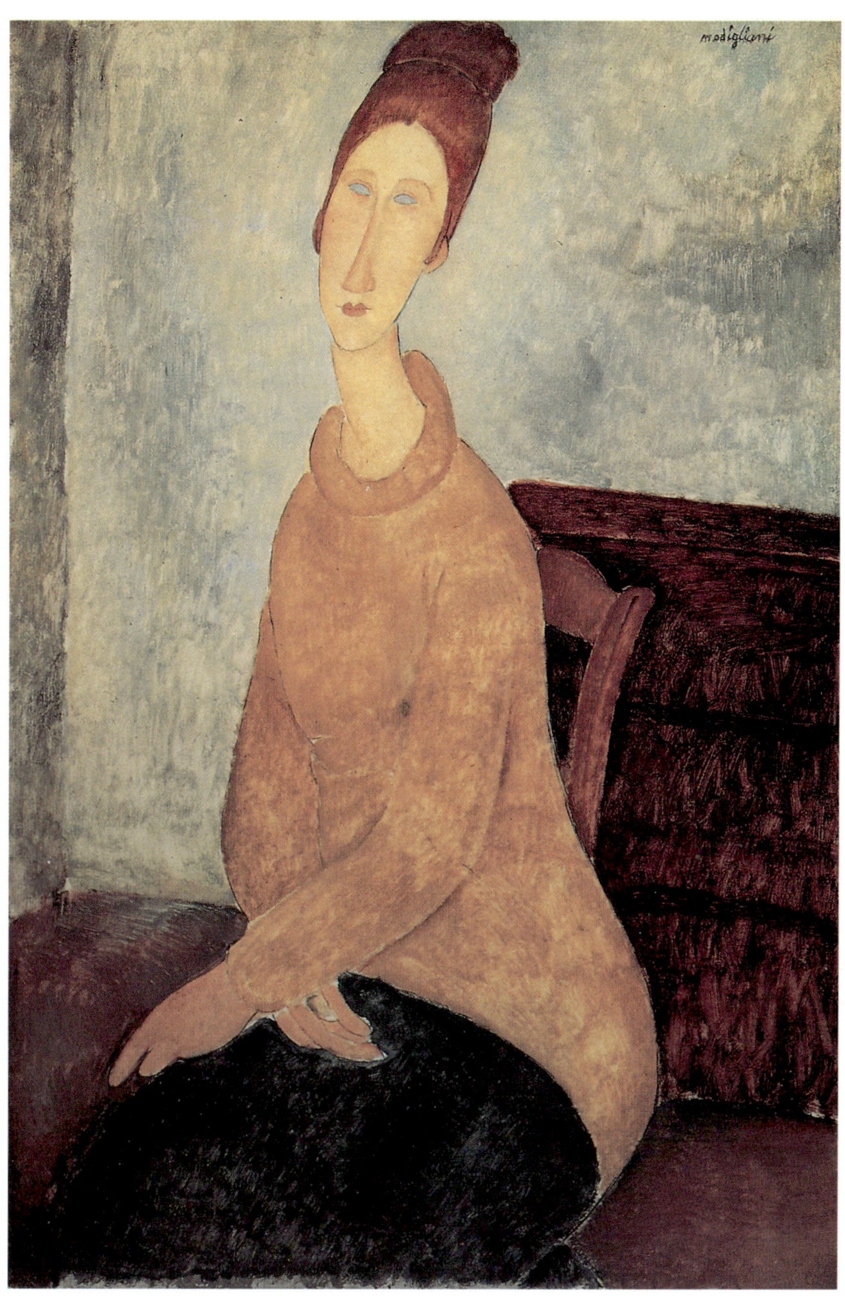

YELLOW SWEATER (PORTRAIT OF MADEMOISELLE HÉBUTERNE), *c.* 1919. Modigliani's friends described his last companion as a talented young artist who, in her lover's presence, always remained imperturbably silent, to the extent that some of those who met her claimed that they never heard her voice. This image of Jeanne Hébuterne —whom her friends used to call "Coconut" for her peculiar auburn hairdo—effectively conveys her gentle and somewhat languorous demeanor. The composition is divided into broad fields of color in a subtly decorative manner; the figure's sinuous silhouette stands out uninterrupted against the background.

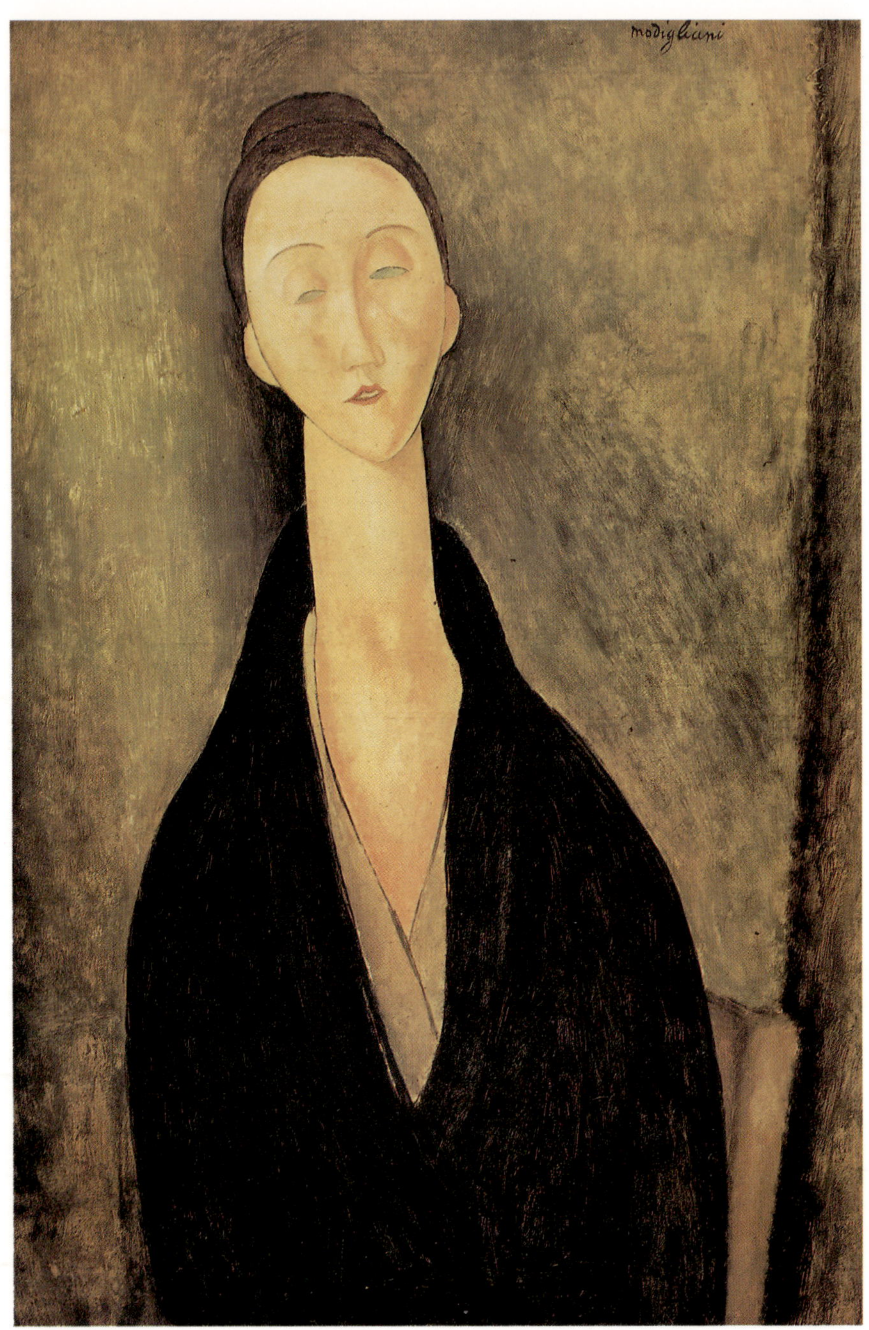

modigliani

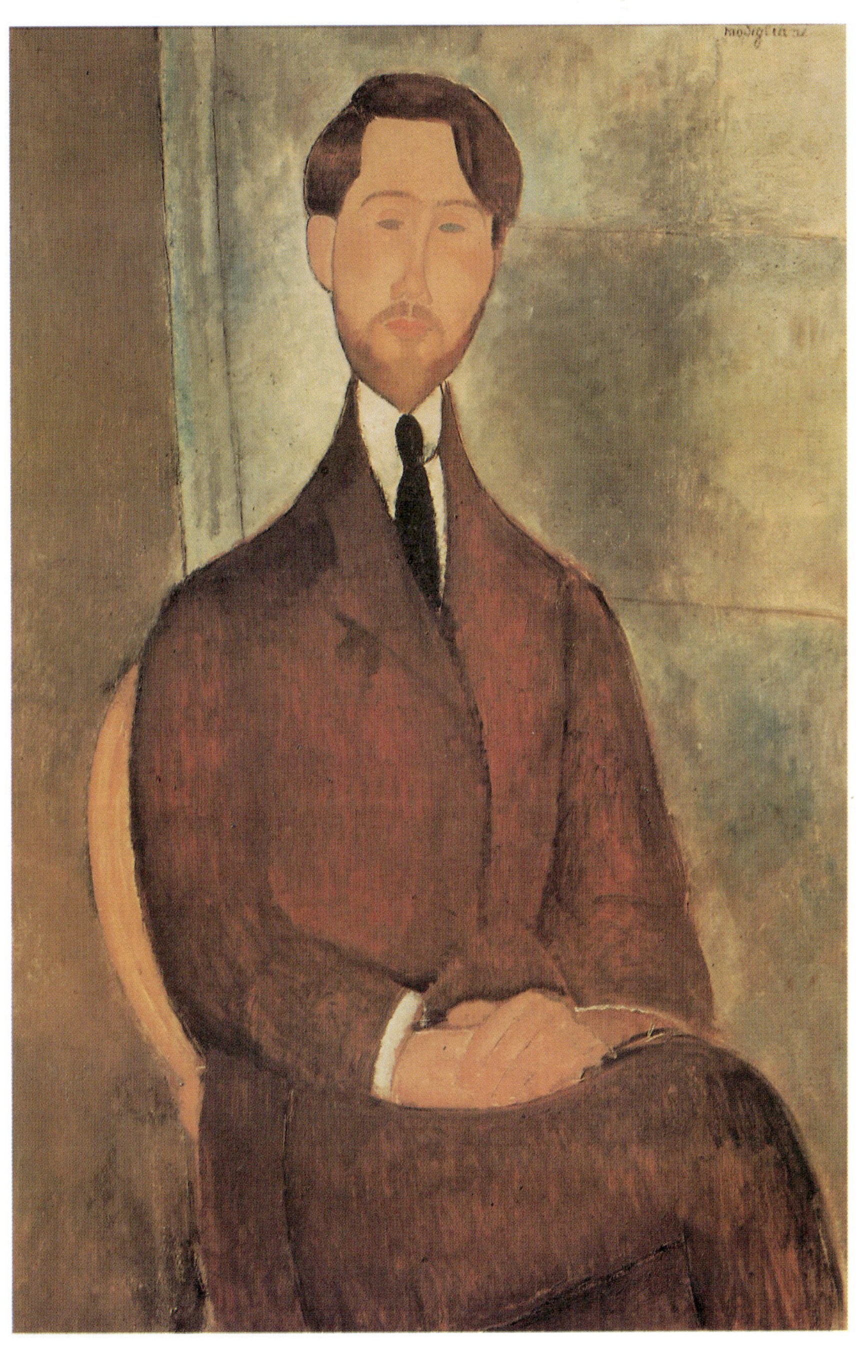

MADAME ZBOROWSKA, 1918; PORTRAIT
OF LEOPOLD ZBOROWSKI, 1919.
In 1916, the encounter between
Modigliani and Leopold Zborowski
marked a turning point in both
of their lives. The painter
found not only a dealer who was
profoundly committed to his
work, but also a friend and a
benefactor. For his part, the
Polish poet decided to give up
literature and, driven by his
obsession for Modigliani's work,
immersed himself completely in
the dealings of the art market.
Their relationship, marked
by the Zborowskis' tireless
devotion to protecting
the artist from his own
intemperance, ended only
with the latter's death.

SELF-PORTRAIT, 1919. In what
was to be one of his last
works, the specter of death
seems to hover over the artist
in his only self-portrait.
Haggard, wasted by disease
and overindulgence, Modigliani
appears to be pondering the
significance of his own métier
as a painter. The end fast
approaching, the artist
portrayed himself with the same
vacant eyes and introspective
gaze found in his other
paintings, trapping himself
and his figures in a similar
state of melancholic detachment.

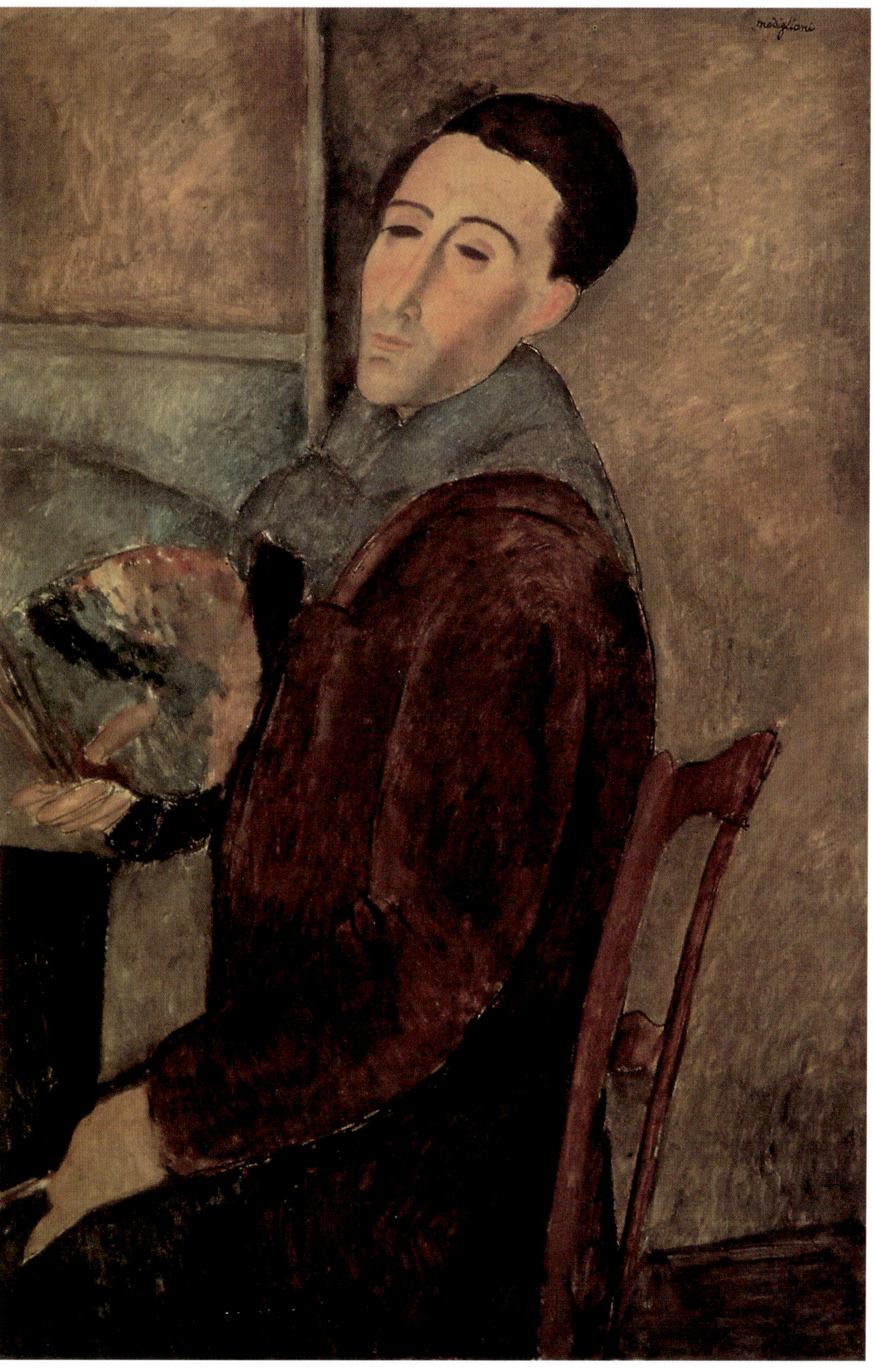

LIST OF WORKS

Seated Caryatid, *c.* 1911.
Pencil on paper.
Private collection.

p 19

Caryatid, *c.* 1911.
Pastel, watercolor, and pencil on
paper, 53 x 43.8 cm.
Musée d'Art Moderne de la Ville de
Paris, Paris.

p 20

Rose Caryatid with a Blue Border,
c. 1913.
Watercolor, 56.6 x 45.1 cm.
Perls Galleries, New York.

p 21

Head of a Woman, *c.* 1911–12.
Sculpture, high 50.8 cm.
Perls Galleries, New York.

p 22

Head, *c.* 1914.
Sculpture, 58 x 12 cm.
Musée National d'Art Moderne,
Centre Georges Pompidou, Paris.

p 23

Caryatid, *c.* 1913–14.
Gouache.
Perls Galleries, New York.

p 24

Caryatid, *c.* 1913–14.
Gouache.
Musée National d'Art Moderne,
Centre Georges Pompidou, Paris.

p 25

Portrait of Frank Burty Haviland,
1914.
Oil on cardboard, 73 x 60 cm.
Private collection, Milan.

p 27

**Preliminary Study for the Portrait
of Diego Rivera,** 1914.
Oil on canvas, 100 x 79 cm.
Museu de Arte, São Paulo, Brazil.

p 28

Antonia, 1915.
Oil on canvas, 82 x 46 cm.
Musée de l'Orangerie, Paris.

p 29

Head of a Young Woman, 1915.
Oil on paper, 54 x 42 cm.
Musée National d'Art Moderne,
Centre Georges Pompidou, Paris.

p 30

**Head of Woman with a Velvet
Ribbon,** 1915.
Oil on canvas, 56 x 47 cm.
Musée de l'Orangerie, Paris.

p 31

The Fat Child (L'Enfant Gras), 1915.
Oil on canvas, 55 x 46 cm.
Private collection, Milan.

p 32

Head of a Woman, 1915.
Oil on canvas, 46 x 88 cm.
Pinacoteca di Brera, Milan.

p 33

Louise, 1915.
Oil on paper, 50 x 37 cm.
Private collection, Milan.

p 34

The Servant, 1916.
Oil on canvas, 73 x 54 cm.
Kunsthaus Museum, Zurich.

p 36

**Portrait of a Young Woman
(Victoria),** 1916.
Oil on canvas, 81 x 60 cm.
The Tate Gallery, London.

p 37

Man in a Hat, 1916.
Oil on canvas, 88 x 45 cm.
Private collection, Milan.

p 38

The Blonde Renée, 1916.
Oil on canvas, 61 x 38 cm.
Museu de Arte, São Paulo, Brazil.

p 39

Head of a Woman in a Hat (Lolotte),
c. 1916.
Oil on canvas, 55 x 88 cm.
Musée National d'Art Moderne,
Centre Georges Pompidou, Paris.

p 40

Head of a Woman with Earrings,
1917.
Oil on canvas, 46 x 30 cm.
Musée National d'Art Moderne,
Centre Georges Pompidou, Paris.

p 41

Woman in a Black Necktie, 1917.
Oil on canvas, 65 x 50 cm.
Private collection, Paris.

pp 42–43

**Woman with Red Hair and Blue
Eyes,** 1917.
Oil on canvas, 55 x 46 cm.
Private collection, Turin.

p 44

Seated Woman (Dédie Hayden), 1918.
Oil on canvas, 92 x 60 cm.
Musée National d'Art Moderne,
Centre Georges Pompidou, Paris.

p 45

Woman with Blue Eyes, 1918.
Oil on canvas, 81 x 54 cm.
Musée National d'Art Moderne,
Centre Georges Pompidou, Paris.

p 46

Young Girl with Brown Hair, 1918.
Oil on canvas, 66 x 45.7 cm.
Private collection, Milan.

p 47

The Little Peasant, 1918.
Oil on canvas, 100 x 65 cm.
The Tate Gallery, London.

p 48

**Young Peasant Leaning Against
a Table,** 1918.
Oil on canvas, 100 x 65 cm.
Musée de l'Orangerie, Paris.

p 49

p 50

Seated Young Woman with Loose Hair, 1919.
Oil on canvas, 116 x 78 cm.
Private collection.

p 51

The Country Girl, 1919.
Oil on canvas, 102 x 65 cm.
Private collection, Paris.

p 53

Seated Nude, 1916.
Oil on canvas, 92 x 60 cm.
The Courtauld Institute of Art,
London.

p 54

Nude on a Cushion, 1917.
Oil on canvas, 60 x 92 cm.
Private collection, Milan.

p 56

Reclining Nude (Le Grand Nu),
1917.
Oil on canvas, 73 x 116 cm.
The Museum of Modern Art,
New York.

p 58

Seated Nude with a Shirt in Her Hands, 1917.
Oil on canvas, 92 x 60 cm.
Private collection, Roubaix.

p 60

Portrait of Hanka Zborowska, c. 1917.
Pencil, 34 x 24 cm.
Private collection.

p 61

Portrait of Aristide Sommat, c. 1918.
Charcoal, 25 x 18.5 cm.
Museo Civico Giovanni Fattori,
Livorno.

p 62

Head of Kisling, 1915.
Oil on canvas, 37 x 28 cm.
Pinacoteca di Brera, Milan.

p 63

Portrait of Beatrice Hastings, 1915.
Oil on paper, 69 x 49 cm.
Private collection, Milan.

p 64

Portrait of Léopold Survage, c. 1917.
Oil on canvas, 61 x 46 cm.
The Art of the Ateneum, Helsinki.

p 65

Portrait of Oscar Miestchaninoff, "Mechan", 1917.
Oil on canvas, 46 x 33 cm.
Perls Galleries, New York.

p 66

Paul Guillaume, "Novo Pilota", 1915.
Oil on canvas, 105 x 75 cm.
Musée de l'Orangerie, Paris.

p 67

Portrait of Paul Guillaume, 1916.
Oil on canvas, 81 x 54 cm.
Civica Galleria d'Arte Moderna,
Milan.

p 68

Portrait of Madame Georges van Muyden, 1917.
Oil on canvas, 92 x 65 cm.
Museu de Arte, São Paulo, Brazil.

p 69

Portrait of Madame Hanka Zborowska, 1917.
Oil on canvas, 55 x 33 cm.
Galleria Nazionale d'Arte Moderna,
Rome.

p 70

Portrait of Lunia Czechowska, 1917.
Oil on canvas, 81 x 45 cm.
Museu de Arte, São Paulo, Brazil.

p 71

Portrait of Jeanne Hébuterne in a Straw Hat, 1917.
Oil on canvas, 55 x 38 cm.
Private collection, New York.

p 72

Portrait of Blaise Cendrars, 1917.
Oil on canvas, 61 x 50 cm.
Private collection, Rome.

p 73

Yellow Sweater (Portrait of Mademoiselle Hébuterne), c. 1919.
Oil on canvas, 100 x 65 cm.
The Solomon R. Guggenheim
Museum, New York.

p 74

Madame Zborowska, 1918.
Oil on canvas.
Museu de Arte, São Paulo, Brazil.

p 75

Portrait of Léopold Zborowski, 1919.
Oil oncanvas, 100 x 65 cm.
Museu de Arte, São Paulo, Brazil.

p 76

Self-Portrait, 1919.
Oil on canvas, 100 x 65 cm.
Museu de Arte, São Paulo, Brazil.

SELECTED BIBLIOGRAPHY

CHRISTIAN PARISOT. *Amedeo Modigliani.* Paris: ACR Editions, 1996.

PIERRE DURIEU. *Modigliani.* Paris: Hazan, 1995.

WERNER SCHMALENBACH. *Amedeo Modigliani: Paintings, Sculptures, Drawings.* Munich: Prestel, 1991.

ALFRED WERNER. *Modigliani.* Paris: Cercle d'Art, 1988.

Modigliani. Catálogo exposición. Barcelona: Centre Cultural de la Caixa de Pensions, 1983.